Everest

Summit of the World

Harry Kikstra

Everest: Summit of the World

First published in 2009 by Rucksack Readers, Landrick Lodge, Dunblane, FK15 0HY, UK
☎+44/0 1786 824 696 web: **www.rucsacs.com** email: info@rucsacs.com

ISBN: 978-1-898481-54-6

Text, design, mapping and layout © Rucksack Readers 2009
Photographs © 2004-2009 **Harry Kikstra**, Rucksack Readers and licensors: see page 95
Additional photography (ten images) © **Alan Arnette**: see page 95
Cartography © WorkHorse 2009: see map flap for sources

The right of Harry Kikstra to be identified as the author of this work has been asserted by
him in accordance with the Copyright, Designs and Patents Act 1988.

All rights reserved. No part of this publication may be reproduced, stored in a retrieval
system, or transmitted in any form or by any means (electronic, mechanical, photocopying,
recording or otherwise) without prior permission in writing from the publisher.

British Library Cataloguing in Publication Data: a catalogue record for this book is available
from the British Library.

Designed in Scotland by WorkHorse **www.workhorse.co.uk**

Colour separation by HK Scanner Arts International Ltd in Hong Kong; printed in China by
Hong Kong Graphics & Printing Ltd

Feedback request
The publisher welcomes comments and updates from readers on any aspect of this book:
please email us at **info@rucsacs.com**.

Disclaimer
An attempt to climb Mount Everest involves risks of personal injury, ill-health
or even death. Readers, even if in excellent general health, should consult their
medical advisers about health issues including high altitude before committing
to any expedition. This book offers information and advice on how to minimize
and manage the dangers. However, every expedition is unique, conditions can
change abruptly and each team is responsible for its own safety. **Neither author
nor publisher can accept any liability for any ill-health, accident or death
arising directly or indirectly from reading this book**.

Although facts have been checked carefully prior to publication, things can
change at any time. You are strongly advised to check the author's website
www.7summits.com for any updates well before you plan to leave.

Contents

Introduction: the seven summits

Denali

Everest's altitude, close to 9 km (5.5
miles), makes it clearly the highest
mountain not only in Asia, but
also in the world. Identifying the
summits of the seven continents is not
straightforward, because there is no
watertight definition of a continent.
The summits of Africa, North and
South America, Antarctica and Asia are
all agreed, but debate persists about
Australasia (Oceania) and Europe.

Equator

If Australia were a continent, then
Kosciuszko would be its summit, but
at a mere 2228m it hardly seems a
worthy member of this global list.
Some stake a claim for Mt Cook in
New Zealand (3754m) or Mt Wilhelm
(4509m) on Papua New Guinea. But
the whole island of New Guinea is
joined to Australia by a continental
shelf, and its Carstensz Pyramid
(4884m) is higher than either, and
offers far more technical challenge.

Aconcagua

continued on p 6

Vinson

Overall difficulty grading

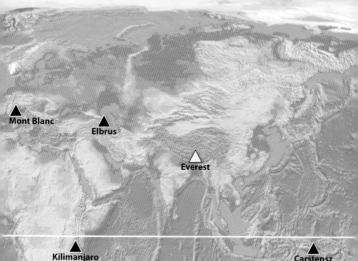

						9000
					Everest	8000
						7000
	Elbrus	Aconcagua				6000
Kilimanjaro			Denali			5000
	Mont Blanc	Carstensz	Vinson			4000
Kosciuszko		Pyramid				3000
						2000
1 2	3	4	5 6	7	8 9	1000 m

Mont Blanc

Elbrus

Everest

Kilimanjaro

Carstensz Pyramid

Kosciuszko

Summary of altitudes and technical difficulty *see page 6*

Continent	Summit	Country	Altitude (metres)	Altitude (feet)	Technical difficulty
Africa	Kilimanjaro	Tanzania	5895	19340	2
Antarctica	Vinson	Antarctica	4897	16065	4-5
Asia	**Everest**	**Nepal/China**	**8848**	**29029**	**7**
Australasia	Carstensz Pyramid	Papua, Irian Jaya	4884	16025	8-9
Australia	Kosciuszko	Australia	2228	7310	1
Europe	Elbrus	Russia	5642	18510	4
Europe, western	Mont Blanc	France	4810	15780	4
North America	Denali (McKinley)	USA	6194	20320	5
South America	Aconcagua	Argentina	6962	22840	3

In 1985, Dick Bass was the first to complete and popularise the seven summits idea (with Kosciuszko). Within a year, Pat Morrow and Reinhold Messner both finished their seven summits with Carstensz Pyramid. Some summiteers nowadays climb both 'just in case'.

By October 2008 the number of completers was 234. Of these, 150 had climbed Carstensz, whereas 179 had chosen Kosciuszko. Altogether 95 completers had climbed both: see ***www.7summits. com/stats*** for an update.

Mont Blanc, the undisputed pinnacle of the Alps, has some claim to be Europe's summit. But Europe's south-eastern boundary is ill-defined, and many people view the Caucasus (where Mount Elbrus lies) as included. To date, nearly all summiteers (including Bass, Morrow and Messner) have chosen Elbrus as their European summit.

The lower table on p5 shows the nine mountains by altitude and technical difficulty, on a scale where 1 means uphill hiking and 9 means hard climbing (rock or ice). But the overall difficulty of climbing each mountain depends on other factors, such as the length of the expedition and how hostile and remote the environment. The graphic atop p5 shows this overall level of challenge, and may help you to plan a sequence for your summit bids. Everest is not the most technical, but its extreme altitude makes it the hardest and most dangerous of all.

1 Planning and preparation
1·1 Planning your trip

Everest is a deadly mountain. Anyone who thinks otherwise has never been there or will never return. It is the hardest of the seven summits, and should certainly be one of the last on your list.

The best preparation for Everest is to complete in advance a series of climbs and courses to train you in all the requirements for a successful climb: extreme physical and mental endurance, winter camping and technical skills in a hostile environment including crevasse rescue, self-sufficiency and rope management. All these must be mastered before landing in Kathmandu. Although you will learn a lot on Everest, think of the climb as a severe and possible fatal final test, not a training ground.

Consider the following:

• A full Everest expedition takes up to two months, and most of that time you will feel unwell, while surrounded only by rocks and ice.
• You cross huge crevasses on treacherous ladders and go from boiling hot to incredibly cold temperatures within hours.
• There is a high risk of frostbite, and you can't count on evacuation.
• Your life is threatened most of the time; if you reach high altitude, you will see and walk past the dead bodies of other climbers.

The reward for all these hardships can be grand. If you reach the summit in decent weather you will become the highest person on Earth, treated to a magnificent view over the Himalayas. And by climbing Everest, or even by just visiting its Base Camps, you get to know the friendly people of Nepal and perhaps also Tibet.

A guided expedition?

All expeditions on Everest are commercially supported, but you choose the extent of the support: basic (permit, transport and oxygen), medium (including food and cooks) or full service (guides, sherpa porter service and a team doctor) or even with flights from your home country. Many variations exist. Although it would be possible to handle every aspect yourself, you would need years of experience and preparation, and may end by paying more.

The team is responsible for the safety of its weakest members: in an unsupported team, first aid expertise and communication skills are vital. If one person becomes seriously ill or has an accident, it's likely to compromise everybody's chance of attempting the summit. This alone makes your chances of summiting greater if you use a guiding service.

Using guides and sherpas has other advantages:

- Although the main routes are obvious, the experts know much more about the specific conditions and how to prepare for them successfully and safely.
- They are responsible for logistics and supplies, leaving you freer to focus on climbing the mountain.
- Because sherpas help to make and break camp, you save energy for your summit bid.

The sherpas are arguably the best guides and many of them have summited many times. Even though almost none of them have UIAGM guide credentials, they know the mountain like no other.

In fact, over 42% of all summits on Everest have been made by Nepali climbers: see p46. Communication may be a problem: not all speak a foreign language well enough to communicate, and small misunderstandings about oxygen or timing can be fatal.

It might be said that if you need a guide for Everest, you are not ready for the mountain. For sure, it's irresponsible to depend too much on one: anybody can fall ill or twist an ankle. In the Death Zone, your guide will also be affected by the altitude: see p14. You should be prepared not only to be self-sufficient, but also to try to help others.

Costs

Any Everest expedition is expensive. Even totally unsupported, you will likely spend close to $10,000 on the Tibet side or $20,000 in Nepal. Once you add the cost of return flights and gear, this can double. A logistical partner can add basic services such as transport, yaks, cooks, tents and food for another $5000-10,000. Commercial 'full service' expedition prices range from $20,000-$50,000 per person in Tibet and from $30,000-$80,000 in Nepal. Allow another few hundred to a few thousand dollars for tips and bonuses to your sherpas, cooks and guides.

You need to plan how to shoulder this huge financial burden. Not dining out, stopping smoking and doing without a car or a big house could save enough to pay for an Everest attempt.

Prices differ enormously. Find out exactly what is included, for safety as well as price comparison. Ask how much oxygen is included (see pp 25-6) and whether you have a personal sherpa, guide and/or doctor. Check also the luggage allowance on the yaks, quality of the food and even the number of tents and radios.

Think carefully where you want to save money: is it worth it saving some money if it means having to share a tent, lacking medical care or eating only freeze-dried food for six weeks?

Theft and pilferage of camps is a growing problem. One friend had his only oxygen bottle stolen, despite being clearly labelled 'emergency oxygen' with his name. Larger expeditions always have spare oxygen, tents, fuel and food available for their clients. But 'budget' climbers often discover too late that they need more resources, and some are tempted to steal what they need.

If asked, the 'big guys' will always help out, but Everest is no supermarket. If you choose to go low-budget, you will have less: it's your choice and you must stick with it. If you get into real trouble, contact the expedition whose gear you need, and ask. Otherwise they may themselves get in trouble later on. Stealing oxygen, fuel or food is not just theft; it can trigger a chain reaction that leads to death. If your action leads to manslaughter, you can be charged accordingly.

Compare prices between different operators, but beware of false economies. Many people have tried to climb Everest on a low budget and failed. If you have to return to try again, you'll need more time off work, further flights and repeat expedition expenses. People have died because of a lack of radio or medical care. Costs can be cut in many ways, but if that means lowering your summit chances or even risking your life, reconsider. Assess also the long-term effects: you may have to quit your job if you can't get time off again, and your partner may lose patience with your passion.

What is the best time of year?

Everest's summit is pounded by the jet stream winds most of the year. Just before and after the monsoon there are periods with less summit wind. This 'weather window' usually opens from late April until early June. Roughly two-thirds of all ascents have been made between 15 and 31 May, so most teams focus on that period.

On the Nepal route, aim to summit in May. In June, warmer weather tends to make the Khumbu Icefall dangerous: see pp 84-5. On the Tibet side, be prepared to summit any time from early May to early June. To allow time to acclimatize, your expedition should start at least 4-5 weeks before your summit attempt. So most expeditions start in late March (from Nepal) or early April (from Tibet).

In autumn there is usually a second period of better weather, and climbers have summited in September and October, accounting for almost 10% of all summits. This period is less fixed and nowadays very few expeditions go then. It is worth considering because:

• You may be alone on the mountain: no circus, no noise, no pollution, no yak-trains.
• The overall weather tends to be better.
• There will be more snow high on the mountain, making the rocky parts (both routes) much easier.

However, there are some drawbacks:

- As your team may be alone, you need to fix all ropes and ladders yourself and there will be no emergency help. This makes it more expensive.
- Each day will be shorter and colder than the previous, and conditions will be tough once you are acclimatized enough for a summit attempt.
- Although the overall weather is usually good, the chance of a weather window is not as strong as in spring. However, there may be a longer period with feasible weather.
- The possible additional snowfall may create avalanche dangers.

Some successful attempts have been made outside these main periods, but those are exceptions: the summer monsoons and the low temperatures and snow in winter usually deter climbers.

Insurance

Make sure that you are insured for rescues and high medical costs. Regular travel insurance policies exclude mountaineering, and even special 'dangerous sports' insurances often exclude altitudes over 6000m. Check the small print carefully: there are large differences between companies in price and cover. Make sure that your expedition leader and Base Camp managers know details such as policy number and contact phone numbers. In an emergency, spending may need to be authorised by the insurers.

Everest (centre) with Lhotse (to its left) from the Pang La

1 Planning and preparation
1·2 Choosing your route

Nowadays, over 96% of all Everest ascents are by the two routes described in this book. Of these, 47% were made by the Tibet route (Part 3) compared with 53% by the Nepal route (Part 4). Both are known by many other names. The *Tibet route* is also known as the *Chinese route*, *North* or *North Col route*, *North-east Ridge route* or the *Mallory route*. The *Nepal route* is sometimes called the *South* or *South Col route*, the *South-east Ridge route* or the *Hillary route*.

Each has its pros and cons. The Nepal route has its biggest dangers relatively low on the mountain: the Khumbu Icefall must be crossed several times, each a Russian roulette, and it leads to a section with many crevasses. If you are ill, getting through the Icefall and down to Kathmandu can be a problem, especially when the weather is too bad for a helicopter. However summit day starts relatively low and is steep and straightforward. All being well, a quick and safe ascent and descent is possible.

Tibet Base Camp can be reached by vehicle, the permit fees are lower and yaks go all the way to Advanced Base Camp, so a full-service expedition can cost less than half. Indeed, the Tibet route has few objective dangers until its final stretch. As a result, an altitude-stricken climber can be evacuated from Advanced Base Camp (ABC) quickly, first on a yak and then in a vehicle from Base Camp (BC). The sections to North Col can be prone to avalanches, but the rest is mainly a high-altitude hike.

However, summit day on the Tibet route is very different: you start high and remain at extreme altitude for a very long time while making the lengthy traverse to and from the summit. This makes the descent much more strenuous than expected. However, the route itself is easy to find: you follow the fixed line from just above ABC to the summit. Also there are three rocky Steps to be climbed on summit day (see pp 69-72), whereas the Nepal route has only one Step, and it's shorter.

The Nepal route is much more expensive due to permit prices, extra services needed for the week-long trek in and because the Icefall barrier stops yak transport from going beyond BC. However, the Khumbu valley trek to BC is attractive and interesting and its many villages have teahouses and lodges, so you can overnight almost anywhere. From BC, the climb is much shorter than on the Tibet side, up fixed lines through the Icefall, across the Western Cwm and then following the ropes to the summit.

As with any high mountain, on both routes you climb many sections repeatedly, ascending to acclimatize, afterwards descending again to rest. Each time you ascend, you go faster: in Parts 3 and 4 we describe each section only once, and show timings to reflect this factor. Within each route we mention some variations, for example in campsites used.

There are many other beautiful mountains in the area, such as Lhotse, Makalu and Pumori. Many aspiring Everest climbers hike as far as Base Camp and climb Kala Pattar, or climb to the North Col, Lakhpa Ri or Island Peak.

Pumori from Camp 2, Tibet route

13

You are engaging in a life-threatening sport: take the disclaimer on page 2 very seriously. Safety depends on your choice of team mates, especially if you don't hire a professional guide or sherpa. If you and your team mates are climbing sensibly, your goal should be that everybody gets back down in good health, whether or not some or all of you reach the summit. There is no summit for which it is worth losing a single finger or toe, let alone risking a life.

The main routes on Everest are often underestimated because they are mostly 'non-technical' routes. But every year, some climbers still die (see p46) and others lose digits to frostbite. You can reduce the risks by acting responsibly and by listening to guides and checking the weather. However, you can never eliminate risk, and you need also to consider the safety of other climbers.

Good communication within the team is vital for a successful expedition. If you are feeling ill or your fingers are numb, it is a sign of strength, not weakness, to be truthful about it. Although team members have a duty to help each other, ultimate responsibility for your own safety belongs to you, not to your team mates or guide.

Death Zone

The upper part of the mountain, usually above 7500m (24,600ft), is referred to as the 'Death Zone' because:

• Your body is slowly dying because of extreme altitude to which humans cannot acclimatize: see p18. Your digestive system slows down, you sleep badly and you use up your reserves. You may lose several kg of body weight per day. Plan to stay in this zone for as short a period as possible, preferably no more than three days.

• If you get into trouble, the chances are very high that you will die. You can't *expect* others to help you. High-altitude rescues are the exception, and they put the lives of the rescuers in severe danger.

- There are dozens of dead bodies both on and near the trail. On Everest, there are relatively few 'classic' accidents such as falls and avalanches. Most climbers die from exhaustion, a heart attack, stroke or the cold, or some combination, while still attached to the fixed rope.

Their bodies are often left, creating a high-altitude cemetery. This is not because of disrespect, but is purely practical. When every step costs all the effort you can muster, there is no way anyone can carry an additional 80-90 kg down over dangerous terrain. And because the air is cold and dry, most corpses are preserved.

Turnaround time

Some groups believe in having a 'turnaround time' – an agreed fixed time for turning back from the summit bid in order to get back down safely. We disagree partly with this idea. A fixed turnaround time can be a dangerous thing. We believe that weather and your team's physical and mental condition should be the deciding factors, not your watch. If the weather is turning bad at 06.00 or you are climbing too slowly or feeling ill, then it is time to turn back, no matter where you are.

There are many people who should have turned back, but continued through harsh weather on legs that would barely carry them, just because it was not yet 'turnaround time'. The mountains and the weather are in charge, not you. Expect to adapt your plans to the conditions. It is important to keep a close eye on the weather. Storms can come in very quickly, with devastating results.

That said, if you are ascending at only 50m per hour and you reach the Second Step or the South Summit 8 hours after leaving High Camp (see p70 and p92), realise that your progress will be much slower from there on, and draw the obvious conclusion. Try to assess your chances objectively. If your team is strong in body and mind, the weather is favourable and you are making good time, keep going. But if any of these factors do not feel right, get down in one piece as soon as possible.

Always be honest with yourself and your team mates. If your first attempt is not set to succeed, conserve your energy and your O_2: see p26. That way you may be able to try again in a week, when you feel better, are more acclimatized or the weather has improved. Make sure you have built flexibility into your schedule, and that this is agreed with your guide and team mates beforehand.

Advance planning checklist

This checklist may help you to plan the months prior to departure:

- consult medical advisor about proposed trip and have a full physical check-up
- plan and execute training programme for fitness, strength and endurance
- register for a climbing permit or commercial expedition
- take out suitable insurance as soon as you book
- weigh all your kit and decide what to replace or upgrade
- organize gear and ship ahead if need be
- check which inoculations are needed and when
- visit dentist for check-up
- consider visit to chiropodist (foot specialist)
- blood donors: last donation no less than 8 weeks before departure.

Planning and preparation
1·4 Altitude effects

The altitude problem is the shortage of oxygen: as you climb
higher, the air gets thinner. At Everest's summit (8848m/29,029ft)
atmospheric pressure is only one third of that at sea level. You
might think that breathing three times faster could compensate,
but the reality is much worse. The lungs' ability to extract oxygen
deteriorates rapidly with altitude – much faster than the decline
in oxygen pressure. Furthermore, when climbing at altitude on
difficult terrain, the body needs more oxygen anyway.

Your heart is the pump that makes your blood circulate. The lungs
load oxygen into your red blood cells for delivery to your muscles
and other vital organs. The oxygen demand from your muscles
depends on their activity level, but your brain also needs its share.
Despite having only 2% of your body weight, your brain needs 15%
of its oxygen. If it gets less, judgement declines, control suffers and
speech can become confused.

Your body responds in various ways to needing more oxygen:
• Right away, you breathe faster and deeper.
• Within minutes, your heart beats faster, sending more oxygen
  to your tissues and forcing blood into parts of your lungs that it
  doesn't normally reach.
• After several days, your body expels excess fluid and starts
  creating more red blood cells, making the blood thicker.
If you find yourself urinating a lot that is a usually a sign that your
body is acclimatizing well. Creating more red blood cells takes at
least a week, and continues over a period.

You can help yourself to acclimatize by breathing deeply and freely,
and by drinking plenty of water. The extremely dry air at altitude,
combined with increased breathing and heart rate, increases the
need for extra water. Drink at least one extra litre per day per
1000m (3300ft) ascended above BC. You may not want to, but force

yourself to drink and eat. It helps to carry a big bottle or thermos and alternate between refills of green tea, water and lemonade.

Sleep is an important time for the body's adjustment: avoid sleeping pills and alcohol, which depress breathing while asleep. However, the best way to avoid altitude sickness is a sensible itinerary and flexibility. Your ally in minimizing its effects is alertness to its symptoms in the whole team.

Although people who normally live at sea level can acclimatize successfully to moderate altitude, the body deteriorates above about 5000m. Most groups try to minimize the number of nights spent above BC and some even descend all the way to the valleys at 4000m to allow recovery before the final summit attempt.

Red blood cells (greatly magnified)

Acute Mountain Sickness is the medical term for altitude or mountain sickness, but 'acute' only means 'sudden-onset'. AMS symptoms, if mild or moderate, often disappear if the victim rests or ascends no further. If AMS is severe, the victim must descend: see below.

Nobody knows how or whether AMS will affect you on Everest. No amount of training, preparation or analysis can predict its effects. Your age and gender affect your chances: females are less likely to experience AMS than males, older climbers less vulnerable than younger ones.

It is essential to be extremely fit to climb Everest, but extreme fitness itself won't protect you from AMS. However, over-exertion is a known risk factor in AMS, and at a given ascent rate, extra fitness should reduce the risk. In practice, however, ultra-fit individuals are more likely to try to ascend too quickly, so end up by making themselves more vulnerable.

Degrees of AMS

The distinctions between mild, moderate and severe AMS are not watertight, but a useful shortcut is provided by the points system, see Table 2.

Mild AMS is common on Everest, and if there are no other symptoms, the ascent can continue. If symptoms persist after taking painkillers and drinking at least a litre of water, or if there is mental confusion or breathing difficulties while at rest, suspect moderate or severe AMS.

Anyone with moderate AMS should be monitored closely in case they worsen. Again, drinking enough water and eating is important. Assess the sufferer's condition first thing in the morning. If symptoms persist after resting, or if there is mental confusion or breathing difficulties while at rest, suspect severe AMS.

Severe AMS is avoidable and treatable, as long as the team is aware of the risks and alert to the symptoms, but it can be life-threatening. Treatment is immediate descent, plus oxygen and suitable drugs where available. The victims' judgement may be affected and they

Table 2: AMS points		Interpretation		
symptom	points	total	*degree of AMS*	treatment
headache	1	1-3	*mild*	drink fluids, pain-killer, rest
insomnia	1			
nausea or loss of appetite	1			
dizziness	1	4-6	*moderate*	drink fluids, pain-killer, no more ascent until better
headache (resistant to pain-killers)	2			
vomiting	2			
breathing difficulty at rest	3			
abnormal fatigue	3	7+	*severe*	emergency medication and immediate descent
low urine production	3			
wet noise when breathing	7			
loss of vision	7			

may deny their symptoms They may show confusion, aggression or apathy. Complications are caused by leakage of fluid into the brain and/or lungs: see the panel opposite.

In severe AMS there may also be *ataxia* – loss of balance and co-ordination – leading to unexpected staggers, stumbles or falls. However, other things can cause ataxia, e.g. extreme cold, tiredness or low blood sugar. Get the sufferer to have a short rest, take a drink and a snack, and put on extra clothing. If he or she recovers promptly, and there are no other symptoms, the ascent can continue.

Listen to the victim's breathing: if there's a crackly, watery noise, suspect HAPE: see panel. Arrange medication and immediate descent.

A Gamow bag is an inflatable tube in which the victim can rest while evacuation is in preparation. Its pressure is raised by pumping and it can save lives.

HACE (see panel) can be treated with Dexamethasone, but first consult a doctor, as it has side-effects and contra-indications.

Complications from AMS (HAPE & HACE)

Edema (or oedema) simply means swelling. HAPE and HACE are serious complications, standing for High Altitude Pulmonary Edema and High Altitude Cerebral Edema. They are caused by swelling of tissues in the lungs and brain respectively. HAPE can occur anywhere above 2500 m and HACE above 3000 m. HAPE has been diagnosed as low as Base Camp (5200 m). Both are more probable at higher altitudes, especially amongst those who ascend quickly, and the two complications can co-exist.

HAPE is caused by fluid from tiny blood vessels leaking into the lungs. It affects perhaps 2% of those at altitude, usually people who already have some AMS symptoms. Cold, exercise and dehydration all increase the risk of HAPE. So does gender: males are 5-6 times more likely to be affected than females, and children are more at risk than adults. Around 10% of HAPE victims will die unless promptly diagnosed and treated.

The HAPE sufferer typically looks and feels ill, and

- has serious difficulty in breathing, which may be noisy, 'crackly' or 'wet'
- is very weak and cannot sustain exercise, not even walking
- has a rapid pulse and perhaps a fever
- may have blue-looking lips, ears and fingernail-beds
- has a cough; if there is pink or frothy sputum, the case is serious.

In HACE, swollen blood vessels in the brain cause pressure to build up, causing symptoms such as ataxia, dizziness, extreme fatigue, vomiting, acute headache, incoherence, hallucinations and numbness. Unless treated promptly – by immediate descent, oxygen and suitable drugs – HACE leads to coma and death.

Summary

To reduce the risk of AMS:

- ascend slowly; climb high, sleep low as far as possible
- drink lots of water
- keep warm, eat regularly and look after yourself.

Be alert for AMS:

- monitor your own and your fellow climbers' acclimatization
- apply the points system to any symptoms: see page 19
- use a pulse oximeter to check your blood oxygen saturation.

Pulse oximeter in action

If AMS strikes:

- if it is mild, try drinking water and taking a pain-killer
- if symptoms persist or are serious, do the above but also rest and don't ascend further
- if symptoms are severe or with complications, get emergency treatment and descend.

Diamox and AMS

Acetazolamide, known by its trade name of Diamox, has been used as a prescription drug for over 25 years (mainly to treat glaucoma), so it has been studied thoroughly. Opinions differ about its use on mountains: some climbers take it routinely as a preventive measure, but many people argue that this is dangerous because it masks symptoms that are better treated by descent. Many teams carry Diamox with them for use in emergencies because it can help to treat AMS.

When you breathe fast or pant, as when exercising at altitude, you lose a lot of carbon dioxide, reducing the acidity of your blood. Diamox blocks or slows the enzyme involved in converting carbon dioxide. As a result, it speeds up acclimatization by stopping the blood from becoming too alkaline and smoothing out your breathing.

Diamox has been known to cause severe allergic reactions in a few individuals. If you plan to take it, try it out ahead of your trip to test if you are allergic, to experiment with dosage and to discover whether you can tolerate the side-effects which may include:

- increased urination (diuresis)
- numbness or tingling in hands, feet and face
- nausea
- finding that carbonated drinks taste flat.

Since altitude has a diuretic effect anyway, many people prefer to avoid Diamox, wishing to avoid further interruptions to sleep in order to urinate. Some doctors feel this is a problem only when dosage is too high; individuals vary so much that you will probably have to establish your own level. Taking Diamox makes it especially important to maintain a high fluid intake.

1 Planning and preparation
1·5 Supplementary oxygen

Supplementary oxygen

Most climbers use supplementary oxygen ('O_2'), carried in bottles and delivered through a face mask. Some feel that using O_2 is 'cheating' as it makes the ascent easier, others regard it as standard equipment, like crampons or gloves. About 4% have summited 'without O_2'. The death rate among them is only slightly higher than for 'O_2' climbers, but most of the 'non-O_2' climbers are far more experienced.

The decision is a personal one, but there are genetic factors to consider. Research shows that most people could not survive a climb of Everest without additional O_2. Most climbers start using it at about 7500m, though some start lower to conserve energy for summit day.

In the Death Zone you can't run around or wave your arms to keep warm: it costs too much energy and oxygen. One reason for using O_2 is that it helps to keep your body warm, preventing frostbite. On the other hand, each system weighs at least 4 kg, not counting spare bottles, so you will need extra energy (and oxygen), just to carry the kit, diminishing its net advantage.

Climbers' oxygen bottles are filled with almost 100% pure O_2. Two systems are in use: POISK which uses constant flow, and the newer Summit which delivers O_2 in pulses. The older POISK system has been tested over many years. It consists of an oxygen cylinder pressurized to several hundred bar and regulator, rubber hose and mask. The cylinder is made of Kevlar-reinforced metal to save weight, and is 3 or 4 litres in volume.

The metal regulator screws on top and it controls the gas flow, measured in litres per minute (l/min). This can be set from 0 to 4 l/min in ½- or 1-litre steps. The display shows pressure remaining. Many factors affect the flow and pressure display, including temperature changes and mechanical errors, so check regularly.

The rubber hose usually has a small flow indicator built in, useful because often it's impossible to check the flow and pressure on the regulator itself, with the display behind you inside your backpack.

The mask itself is held over your face with an elastic band. Although it protects your face against frostbite, it also limits your view and can fog your goggles. It has a rebreather bag on the side, which re-uses your exhaled CO_2 and some of the moisture you exhale.

The Summit system replaces the big POISK mask with small plastic tubes for your nose, leaving your mouth and vision free. Summit delivers oxygen in pulses, activated by the lower pressure when breathing in. A bottle will thus last much longer, so less weight has to be carried.

The disadvantage is that Summit depends on electronics and batteries which die quickly in the cold. It could still work as constant-flow, but you'd then have to bring extra bottles anyway. Also the plastic tubes may fill with mucus, may freeze and get blocked easily. Most climbers stick with POISK.

Whichever system you use, check that:

• the bottles are from a reputable supplier, preferably direct from the factory. Some organizations re-fill their bottles to save costs, but the oxygen content and quality could be compromised.

• Open the regulator fully before screwing it onto the bottle and close it only when the oxygen is flowing through it. Some regulators have broken because of sudden high pressure when attached 'closed' to a pressurized bottle.

POISK system

- Long before you need oxygen, test how the regulator and mask work together. Read the pressure, then let the oxygen flow at a fixed rate for several minutes, timed carefully. Check the remaining pressure and calculate the actual flow. Compare it with the flow rate shown on the gauge. You won't get 100% accuracy because temperature changes or defects can cause fluctuations. But knowing if your regulator under- or over-delivers means you can calculate your remaining O_2 time better.
- Ensure that you have enough. Although using O_2 can increase safety, if it runs out, the sudden shock can be deadly, especially if you were using a high flow rate.

Graph of remaining oxygen time (4-litre bottle)

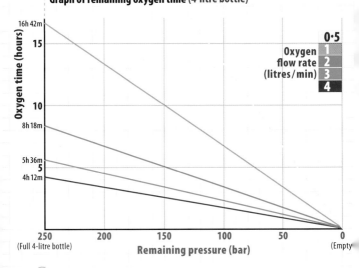

Calculating remaining oxygen time

To find how much oxygen is in a bottle, multiply its volume in litres by its pressure in bar. The normal size is 4 litres, but 3-litre bottles also exist: check carefully and multiply by ¾ for the smaller size.

A 4-litre bottle at 250 bar ('full') effectively holds 1000 litres of O_2 at atmospheric pressure (1 bar). At 200 bar it holds 800 litres, and so on. Although bottles may be factory-filled to 300 bar, by the time they are ready to use, leakage and cold reduce this to about 250 bar. The pressure can vary by up to +/-15%, so always check the gauge.

How long the oxygen in your bottle will last depends on
a) how much it holds now (volume x pressure)
b) the flow rate you set, in litres per minute.

For example you'll set a flow of 0.5 l/min while sleeping or resting in high camps, but more, perhaps 2 to 3 l/min, when climbing. For short periods, e.g. the steepest parts of the Hillary or Second Step, you may need maximum flow (4 l/min). At that setting, a full 4-litre bottle would last only 1000/4=250 minutes – just over 4 hours.

Use the graph opposite to read off remaining oxygen time at a given flow rate (coloured lines) for a given pressure (horizontal axis).

To complicate things, temperature affects oxygen pressure. It can also affect the regulator flow rate unexpectedly. The most accurate measurement would be to weigh the bottle, since the mass of the oxygen it contains stays constant. Since weighing isn't feasible, you need to monitor your gauge and manage your supply carefully.

A higher flow rate means you feel better and climb faster. However, you need more bottles, and carrying extra loads increases your oxygen need. Each climber must find the best balance.

As a guideline, most people use at least 4-5 bottles per attempt:

- One bottle covers a night at Camp 2 and a move to High Camp, where you can start a second bottle if need be.
- A second bottle (perhaps partly used) stays in High Camp for emergency and descent.
- Summit day: maximum of three bottles, even if you have a personal sherpa to carry two of them for you. Reckon on up to 18 hours of oxygen time, either as 6 hours each with 3 bottles or 9 hours each with 2 bottles. Allowing for briefly increased flow for strenuous sections, that means a flow rate of either 2 l/min or 1.5 l/min depending on whether you have 3 bottles or 2. (This assumes that all bottles are 4 litres and filled to 250 bar. Use only full bottles on summit day.)

To save energy, many climbers start using O_2 from about 7000m, so they need at least one further bottle. Always mark your bottles clearly, with waterproof markers and stickers. This may prevent 'accidental' usage by other climbers, a growing problem on Everest.

If you feel really bad on a summit attempt, it's better to give up early. That way you can rest, recover and may be able to try again, whereas if you've used too much precious oxygen, your bid is over.

In summary, the benefits of O_2 are higher climbing speed and warmer body temperature. Its drawbacks are its weight and your dependency.

Climbers just above the Third Step, Tibet

The Khumbu Cough

This infamous condition is prevalent on both sides of the mountain, at any altitude from BC upward, and is caused by constant exposure to cold, dry air. Especially when breathing fast, the lung tissue and bronchi are irritated. The dry and very persistent cough can take so much energy that it leaves you drained and unable to climb. Also its forcefulness can tear muscles and tendons, or even crack ribs!

The Khumbu Cough is not a bacterial infection, so antibiotics don't help (although useful in case of lung infection). Here is how to prevent and treat it:

- Cover your mouth as much as possible while hiking, climbing and even sleeping. Use at least a cheap surgical or builder's mask, or even a scarf or bandana. Specialized masks have small metal frames and special 'beaks' so as to trap heat and moisture from exhaled breath and transfer it back to incoming air.
- If you feel you can't get enough air, you are probably going too fast: slow down and/or rest.
- Try to control your exercise level, avoiding sudden increases in breathing rate.
- Hydrate: drink a lot of water and hot drinks to soothe your system. Check the colour of your urine daily: if it is darker than straw colour, drink more, even if it means getting up at night.
- Suck on throat sweets or candy all day long.

Take extra vitamin C, which is good for general resistance anyway. Experts suggest between 2-5 grams per day extra in the mountains. Any excess will be excreted and may make your urine look yellower.

Food and hygiene

If you are not packing your own food, make sure you communicate any dietary restrictions or allergies to your tour operator, cook and guide. Make a list of any forbidden items and check with your guide/cook. Give special thought to food for summit day: pack snacks that are energy-rich but easy to digest and manageable even when frozen.

Personal hygiene is important. Clean your hands before touching anything you may eat or drink from. Use anti-bacterial wet wipes or wash in hot water in a container if the weather is good, discarding the water well away from any stream or area of snow used for melting. Be careful after shaking other climbers' hands, as there can be many viruses from all over the world amongst the range of nationalities. Even a simple cold can ruin your summit attempt.

Use the toilet tents wherever available. Higher up, be sure to use the same area as all other climbers. This will limit the impact on nature as well as keep the pollution in one obvious spot, making it easier to avoid when collecting clean snow for melting.

Remember that climbers have perished by stepping away from their tent to relieve themselves and losing their balance. Make sure you are in a safe place, or else stay connected to the rope and wear crampons where needed. In extreme conditions, or on difficult terrain, it may be safer to defecate in the vestibule of your tent, especially at night.

Sun protection and snow-blindness

Sunburn is an unexpectedly serious hazard. It's easy to under-estimate the fierce UV radiation when your skin is cold, as at altitude. Especially in the approach days, your surroundings can feel like an oven due to all the reflected sunlight. If it's windy you will feel cold, but you need to take extra care not to get burned.

Bring the strongest sun block you can find, and apply and re-apply it regularly to all exposed skin. Always wear something on your head to prevent heatstroke, and use glacier glasses with a nose-piece, as well as side-pieces. Keep your mouth covered: it's easy to get burned inside your mouth by reflected radiation.

Beware of the danger of snow-blindness – in effect, sunburn of the cornea. You may not realise it at the time, but next day your eyes will be very painful, as if someone is rubbing sand in. You may not be able to open them for a day or two, leaving you effectively blind.

Prevention is simple, but vital. Always wear specialized UV filtering glacier glasses or ski goggles. Regular glasses without side-shields may enlarge your irises, helping the UV rays to damage your eyes. Even if the sky is covered with clouds, the risk is almost as great. Don't forget eye protection when leaving in the dark for the summit.

Signs of the onset of snow-blindness are red and weeping eyes and a 'sandy' sensation. If you have become snow-blind, try to cover your eyes for at least 24 hours to protect them from any further UV exposure. If possible, rinse them a few times daily with water that has been boiled and cooled. Ease the pain with a cold compress, regular painkillers or specialized snow-blindness drops.

Eyes and nose are very vulnerable

Frostbite

Everest is extremely cold, and wind chill makes it feel even colder. Due to your low speed it is very hard to get warmed up again through activity, so try to start warm. Always protect your hands, head and feet, and drink plenty of water. Garlic and aspirin help to keep your blood free-flowing, reducing the risk of frostbite.

If at any time you can't feel your toes or fingers, warm them in any way possible. If wriggling your toes doesn't work, try to put your feet on the belly or in the armpits of a fellow climber. Don't be ashamed of doing this, or of descending if you can't get warm again. Losing a toe or finger is a much greater shame.

You won't feel it when your flesh freezes, only when it thaws again. Check your team mates' faces as well as your own. If you have frostnip (light frostbite) on your hands or feet, warm them in lukewarm water if possible. If any tissue becomes frozen, it's very important not to let it thaw and refreeze. See a doctor as soon as possible for proper treatment.

Summit fever

This is a real disease and probably the main cause of death on Everest. It does not discriminate by age, sex, nationality or wallet size. Many weeks of relative isolation and mental and physical exhaustion combined with lack of oxygen and experience can cloud your judgement.

After all the mental and physical challenges *before* departure, climbers have withstood nearly two months of doubts, pain and temptation. Now, for the first time, the goal that started all this misery – probably years ago – is actually in sight. This can bring on a dangerous euphoria.

People may feel they have 'earned the reward' and may ignore clear warning signs such as numb fingers or oncoming bad weather. That elusive summit seems like something that can be reached, must be reached. The lack of oxygen makes it hard to focus on anything else: the view has narrowed to a single point. Risks that would be opposed whole-heartedly at sea level are now accepted without question.

It can be very hard to evaluate conditions and priorities objectively. The body and mind are connected only loosely. The first time you attempt Everest you are at higher altitude than ever before. Your body wants you to turn back, but your mind is telling you that you are supposed to feel bad and tries to make your body continue.

This may result in failing to recognize extreme exhaustion or freezing body parts. Instead of trying to conserve energy for the way down, you are tempted to spend all your reserves on reaching the summit. A finger suddenly seems a small price to pay compared with the physical and mental pain already endured. Your world may shrink until it seems to contains only you. You may even think 'each one for himself, I deserve it'. Your conscience will make you pay off this high-interest loan for a long time after coming down again.

The possibility of summit fever is the main reason not to climb alone or even unsupported. Try to contact your team mates or leader before making any major decision.

There is only one true goal in climbing: to come back alive. You have more important things waiting for you at home. The summit is just a block of ice on a patch of rock. Turning back, or helping somebody else instead of summiting, is no defeat. It shows wisdom and experience. You will still have a clear conscience and the rest of your life to share with your loved ones.

Physical and mental training

In order to climb Everest, you need to be very healthy and extremely fit, with your heart and lungs especially in top condition. Summit day feels like running a triple marathon with weights on your feet, while breathing through a straw and fighting a migraine. And that challenge comes after two months of continuous physical and mental exhaustion.

Start training as soon as possible, at least 9-12 months before the climb. Preparation is literally vital: your life will depend on it. Focus on aerobic exercise, such as running and cycling, combined with hiking. Steadily work up to training for many hours as a time, and progressively towards training for several days in a row to increase stamina. Brush up on your rock-climbing and rope skills. Although you will not need them for protracted periods, the times when you depend on your skills are literally vital.

Almost all climbers (even those in 'unsupported expeditions') have their gear portered or trucked up to BC and even to ABC or higher. Even though very few climbers carry heavy loads themselves, strengthen your muscular skeleton and especially your back and abdomen. Do not 'bulk up' your muscles: bodybuilders don't do well on Everest. Climbers need efficient muscles, not big ones that use up extra oxygen.

There is no optimum age for this mountain. Experience and maturity can partly offset extra fitness in younger climbers. Imagine being locked up in an inhospitable place for several weeks, without any trees or even natural colours. Every day you feel bad, and the moment you feel a bit better, you move higher and start feeling bad again. You are surrounded by sick people, and climbers whom you met only last week die climbing. Simple tasks become onerous, and the expedition becomes an odyssey with a possible fatal outcome. Most of the time, climbing Everest is no fun.

If you aren't prepared for non-stop mental exhaustion, then your mind will make your body unwell. If you don't *really* want to summit Everest, you won't stand a chance. Experience gained on previous expeditions is invaluable, both for technical expertise and mental strength. Still, some aspects will be new.

You can't summit without stepping over dead climbers along the way. Most of them thought that it would not happen to them, but it did. Are you 100% ready for Everest?

Experience

What if you lose your descender at the top of the Second Step, would your oxygen-deprived brain know how to make an HMS/ Munter hitch knot? If you feel ill, will you go to sleep or force yourself to drink more first? Would you know when your toes or fingers are numb and about to freeze?

On Everest, basic mountaineering skills and knowledge need to be instinctive. You have no spare mental capacity to think out solutions. If you are not very experienced yet, start with basic mountaineering courses. Learn and learn more. Then slowly make your way up higher and colder mountains. The other six of the 'seven summits' are great training, so you'll already have experienced most aspects of an Everest climb.

Then you need to tackle a longer expedition at high altitude, so climb another 8000+ peak, such as Cho Oyu, Broad Peak or Shishapangma. Don't underestimate any of these. They are dangerous giants in their own right.

1 Planning and preparation
1·8 Equipment and packing

You need to plan your gear far ahead. From previous expeditions to high, cold mountains, you probably already have most of the clothing that you need, including a down jacket and lots of layers of breathable clothing to allow for the extreme range of temperatures. However, Everest expeditions involve some special factors:

- Being oxygen-starved makes it hard for your body to keep warm by exercise. And at night, you'll be sleeping on snow and ice in extreme conditions: see below.
- During the many acclimatization climbs, your gear will be scattered between camps and you'll need at least two full sets of basic gear. (You could arrange to share sleeping bags and tents between team members, but this needs careful planning.)
- Certain gear is already included in the services that you book: check carefully with your organizer or expedition leader.

Below is some general advice, but please download our comprehensive packing list from **www.7summits.com/everest**

Essential warm clothing includes

- full **down suit** to keep you warm even at rest. Consider ease of going to the toilet before choosing a suit. Also check it has full ventilation zips to prevent sweating/dehydration.
- high-altitude **expedition boots**, with integrated supergaiter, rated to at least -30° C. Make sure there's plenty of room for warm socks and for toes to wriggle: your feet may expand at altitude, and so may the inner boot foam.
- very warm **gloves and mittens**: gloves are better for rope-handling, but take down mittens, which are warmer, as back-up. Bring thinner windproof and waterproof gloves for the first weeks.
- **face protection**: a full-face windblock balaclava may save your ears and face from frostbite. A mask can help to prevent the Khumbu Cough: see p27.

- very warm **sleeping bag and mattress**: without excellent overnight kit, you won't sleep well, and this alone could prevent you from reaching high altitude. The bag should be rated to at least -29° C (-20° F) and preferably colder – e.g. -40 to -50° C (-40 to -58° F). Even if you sleep in your down suit to save weight, you'll need a light bag and down booties. Underneath, you need a self-inflating air mattress, with a closed cell mat to go beneath.

A tent of your own

Climbing Everest is more than just a mountain trip. You are relocating to a different place for several months. Because you will be surrounded by strange people and a different culture, you may find your need for a temporary 'home' even stronger. A private BC tent may be a necessity, rather than a luxury, to provide you with a place to rest mentally as well as physically. It needs enough space to be your home, to contain your clothes, snacks, music and books and maybe even pictures or gifts from your loved ones.

Sending stuff ahead

If you fly in to Kathmandu, your full kit is likely to be too heavy. To avoid excess baggage fees, you can ship items as cargo well in advance. For shipping and yak transport, the best way to pack the gear is in hard plastic drums, although duffel bags are more useful when in camp. Contact your organizer for detailed shipping instructions and email them a detailed list with number, weight and value of all goods so they can clear Nepali customs for you.

Repacking in Kathmandu

Check with your organizer about the logistics and services included (number of porters and yaks). You'll need to split your gear in two parts: the greater part is what you need only for BC and above. For the approach to BC your stuff should fit in a rucksack or duffel bag, with maybe also a daypack. Bring at least a sleeping bag, windproof and waterproof clothes, down jacket, socks and underwear for a week. Also, carry your camera and electronics with chargers. While in BC, you'll need to repack for the higher camps.

Visas, permits and Liaison Officers

Almost all expeditions start in Kathmandu, Nepal, even those climbing from Tibet. A visa for Nepal can be obtained on entry. For climbing in Tibet it may be cheaper to buy two single-entry Nepal visas than a multiple-entry: bring two passport photos. You'll also need a Chinese visa. Your local organizer normally handles Chinese visas and climbing permits.

The Nepalese permit is very expensive – $10,000 per climber in 2008 – and it confers only permission to climb above BC. All other services (such as porters, yaks, and transportation) cost extra. Commercial organizers offer permits and services as a package, which saves a great deal of time and effort. Even for an 'unsupported' climb, use a Nepalese trekking agency. Prepare your expedition well ahead of time. (Trekkers to Nepal BC only pay a small Sagarmatha National Park fee at Monjo.)

The Tibetan permit is cheaper and includes basic services, with options to add further resources. In 2008 about $7500 paid for transport, accommodation and food from Kathmandu to Tibet BC including climbing permit and yak transport to ABC. Although the Chinese Tibetan Mountaineering Association (CTMA) is responsible for permits, the Nepalese trekking agencies will handle them.

A Liaison Officer (LO) is involved in every expedition: in Nepal, an LO is assigned to each team, whereas in Tibet the LO watches from his stone penthouse all the time, and pays unexpected visits. Some of the LOs seem to want to frustrate your progress, whilst others do their utmost to be helpful. You may need their help for additional services, to bend the rules or even for a rescue. Being friendly works best.

Note that separate permits are needed for any commercial filming, and also, depending on the mood of the LOs, for the use of large video cameras. Costs range from $5000 in Tibet to $1200 in Nepal. Such permits may be revoked without notice.

Sanitary and waste

A deposit is paid to ensure that you'll take your trash away from the mountain, including empty oxygen bottles as well as human and food waste. Responsible climbers would do this anyway, avoiding litter and 'biodegradable' trash which may never decompose in the cold dry air. Ensure that your team mates, cooks and yak herders all help to keep the mountain pristine.

Weather

The infamous 'plume' blowing off the summit isn't snow, but condensation. It indicates summit wind, which can be ferocious even when the sky is clear and lower camps are becalmed. In the BCs it usually freezes at night, but can be hot during the daytime. Be careful to drink enough to prevent sunburn and dehydration.

In general, wind is the showstopper. Entire camps have been destroyed by sudden storms. You may get very hot while climbing, but temperature and pressure can drop very fast. So always be prepared and don't get caught between camps without proper clothes and protection.

Storms can bring heavy snowfall and sudden white-outs that destroy visibility: stay close to the fixed rope. Lower down the mountain, on the rocky trails, snow can cover the track in moments: know your way and note the landmarks.

Use weather forecasts, though not all are accurate and they may be costly. You'll need access to a computer or satphone to receive updates. Co-operate with other teams and compare their forecasts. Always be prepared for sudden change. From the start of your summit bid, at least three days will pass before you approach the top. Conditions can change meanwhile, so stay in contact and always be prepared to turn back.

Iridium
satphone

Radios, satphones and laptops

Bring several means of communication, but don't count on them to get you out of trouble, or even to work! CB radios are useful to hear from team mates, other groups and to receive weather forecasts. Note that these radios normally need a clear line of sight. Moving a few metres can make all the difference to reception.

Have a fixed radio frequency for your team that no other team is using. Don't use a general frequency for chit-chat lest you interfere with safety conversations. Set fixed times to call in to (A)BC, so they know that climbers are OK. Write the times on a piece of tape and attach it to the handsets.

Cell phones may work on the Tibet side – the Chinese have placed a GSM mast at Rongbuk – but using a satphone is likely to be cheaper. The Thuraya satellite system generally works best because it's geostationary: once the satellite is found, you stay connected. The handsets are also smaller, but the service occasionally disappears unexpectedly. The alternative Iridium system has seen fewer outages, but because its satellites aren't geostationary, line of sight is easily blocked and calls may be dropped.

For all equipment, be sure to bring spare batteries and keep them warm. Although satellite phone calls are generally much cheaper than GSM roaming, the data options – sending/receiving images and reports – can cost a fortune, so check the tariffs.

Nowadays laptops are often taken to Everest, at least to the BCs, but about half of them fail. Many never recover, so back up data before and during the trip. The biggest threat for a laptop (and older MP3 players) is low pressure making hard disks crash. Most are not designed for altitudes above 3000m/10,000ft. New solid state hard disks work better because they have no moving parts.

Note that bringing a satphone or a laptop to keep your family informed can be counter-productive: your home team will get worried when they cannot reach you or hear nothing from you. Explain that equipment and service can fail in many ways. No news, perhaps for days or even weeks, is good news.

Rescue

If someone becomes ill or has an accident, rescue may be needed. Some conditions demand only a quick descent, whilst others require urgent hospital care. *Where* the trouble starts is crucial. Up to BC you can usually be evacuated relatively easily: on the Tibet side, go to the LO's house to arrange a vehicle. In Nepal, rescue is by helicopter, yak or porter, but helicopters need excellent weather to fly.

In Tibet the yaks can go all the way up to ABC for evacuations, but it's a long way down to BC, so rescue is slow. From ABC in Nepal you descend through the Icefall, which can be very slow and dangerous.

Above ABC, and especially on summit day, you can't count on a rescue. Rescue helicopters can't fly that high, nor yaks reach the upper parts. Your team and perhaps other climbers may help in an emergency, but they may be in trouble themselves, may have summit fever (see p30) or may not know you're having problems.

If you are in trouble:

- Stop climbing. Your summit attempt is over: get down as fast as possible.
- Tell your team leaders in (A)BC where and how you are, and take their advice seriously. Keep them updated so they can prepare further treatment and/or evacuation and contact your insurers.
- Take good care of yourself: keep drinking, keep warm (but minimize sweating), reapply sunscreen and wear sunglasses. Many victims suffered extra problems such as snow-blindness or dehydration needlessly.
- Stay awake and continue to descend. Take short rests, but don't sleep, however much you want to.

Every climber in the Death Zone is already, in a sense, dying, making it difficult to recognize a really serious situation. Experience helps climbers to know what is life-threatening. If you are not experienced enough, climb with someone who is (sherpa, guide or fellow climber).

Even unsupported teams should have members with extensive medical knowledge and experience. If not, then at least know the radio frequencies of bigger expeditions with dedicated doctors whom you can contact for help.

Food, snacks and supplements

On a long expedition, it is vital to eat well in quantity and in quality. Great food may seem tasteless at altitude or if you are ill. You may have to force yourself to eat regularly lest you lack the energy for a successful climb. In addition to snacks, carry also multivitamins (see p27 re Vitamin C). Carry also garlic pills, to help to prevent frostbite, and Ginkgo biloba, said to improve concentration and to combat altitude sickness.

When selecting an expedition or logistics provider, ask them how they organize re-supply and do they have fresh fruit, vegetables or meat? Ask previous clients where possible. Any organizer that saves money on food is not taking their clients' welfare seriously.

In the Death Zone your appetite may be non-existent and digestion poor. So make sure you eat well before your summit attempt. Don't carry too much heavy food to the highest camps. Most climbers eat nothing there, or stick to simple dehydrated pasta and soups, combined with power gels, biscuits and chocolate.

Packing and yaks

Yaks are hardy animals, and an indispensable part of daily life in the region. On the Nepal side, yaks carry supplies and luggage all the way to BC. In Tibet they are used for the long stretch between BC and ABC.

You'll see a lot of slow-moving 'yak-trains': long lines of yaks, carrying big duffel bags, gas bottles, drums and even their own food. A few herders control the animals by shouting and throwing rocks.

Yaks are nervous. Their approach is announced by the sound of their bells and the herders' shouts. Step off the track to let them pass: if on a slope, walk uphill a bit ahead of them and then stand still to avoid scaring them. In panic, yaks have pushed climbers off the track, lost their loads, or even been killed after moving off the track and slipping. Protect yourself, as well as them, by giving them space.

Use strong waterproof duffel bags to pack your gear and plan wisely. Don't pack any breakable items for yak transport unless wrapped very carefully inside plastic drums. Note that most drums are not only waterproof, but also airtight. This means that drums packed at low pressure in ABC or BC may be seriously dented when unpacked in the higher atmospheric pressure of Kathmandu.

Yaks provide hardy, essential transport

Ropes and ladders

Every season, a team of sherpas fixes a new, different-coloured rope from BC (Nepal) or ABC (Tibet) to the summit. It is mostly two-way traffic, using a single line for both directions. Where there is a separate descent line, never go up it or you will obstruct climbers coming down. Depending on the terrain, the ropes are fixed every 10-50 metres with anchors and there may be knots between anchors as well. When going up, make sure you use a back up carabiner as well as an ascender. Attach both to the strongest safety loop of your harness with a schling/tube-webbing.

When coming to an anchor point or knot:

• Don't move your ascender all the way to the knot or you won't be able to get it off the rope: stop a few cm before.

• First move your back-up carabiner past the knot or anchor.

• Then remove the ascender from the rope and immediately attach it again to the rope, just after the carabiner. This way you will always be attached to the ropes, providing protection even if you slip when moving the ascender.

Use the rope only as a passive guide or safety line, don't pull on it. This disturbs other climbers on the same stretch, pulling them off balance. Also the ropes are damaged by exposure to UV light, rockfall and crampons, and they have been wet and refrozen many times. For every visible broken part, there will be lots of invisible weak spots. The anchors can also work loose, so minimize the stress on them. Use your ice axe and crampons and walk up the slopes, avoiding stepping on the ropes with your crampons.

Crevasse crossing by ladder

When descending you should also be attached to the rope, but ascenders are of little use when going down. On relatively flat parts you can brake by wrapping the rope around your glove and underarm. Always wear gloves and have your ice-axe in your other hand. On steeper parts you need to use a descender, for example a figure-of-eight or stitch plate.

On the Tibet side there are normally only a few ladders. On the Nepal side there are lots, spanning countless crevasses ranging from 1 to 12 metres wide. In places, two or more ladders are tied together. Usually at least one rope is fixed close to the ladder: use it like any other fixed rope. If there is a second rope stretched, fix your back-up carabiner to it; otherwise connect it to the first rope as well.

The ladders are flexible and will sag a bit when you cross. If you have shaky legs, the ladder can pick up a sideways motion which can increase alarmingly. If so, stop and wait until it dies out before continuing. Avoid stepping on the ropes that bind ladders together. Your crampons will damage the ropes, and could get entangled. A slow but steady pace is the key.

Ladders can be at any angle from horizontal to vertical, presenting varying climbing difficulties. If the slope of the ladder is less than 45 degrees, then it's usually easier to stand up and walk while holding the ropes for balance only. If it is steeper, try grabbing the rungs with your hands. Move only one hand or foot at a time to maintain balance. Aim for a steady pace, and don't rush lest you get dizzy and lose your balance.

The ladders should be secured at both sides, but as their anchors are placed in snow and ice, they can melt and the ladder can sink in. Always check carefully and test before placing your full weight on them. Crossing a ladder is always safer early in the day, while it is still cold. Remember that the whole area is dangerous, especially the sections *between* ladders.

The name

In 1852, Surveyor-General Andrew Waugh was told by his British Ordnance Survey of India team that 'Peak XV' had been measured at more than 29,000 feet and was the world's highest mountain. He tried to find a local name, but failed to get consensus, so instead he called it after his predecessor, Colonel George Everest. Waugh reported its name, location and height (29,002 ft) to the Royal Geographical Scoiety in 1856.

In the Tibetan and Sherpa language, the mountain is called *Chomolungma* (Qomolangma), meaning *Mother of the Universe* or *Goddess Mother of the Earth*. Only 50 years ago, the Nepali Government officially named the mountain Sagarmatha, *Goddess of the Sky*, even though the Nepali sherpas also call her *Chomolungma*.

Summit height

In 1955, Everest's snow-cap was re-measured by Indian surveyors and found to be 8848m (29,029ft) – a figure confirmed by Chinese scientists in 1975. In 1999, Bradford Washburn led a cartographic team using GPS, but their height of 8850m (29,035ft) has never been accepted by the Nepali nor the Chinese.

In 2005 the Chinese summited with a large team and made precise measurements using the latest technology. The new rock-height was announced as 8844.43m ± 0.21m, plus 3.5m of snow and ice on top. The sum matches the previous figure of 8848m (29,029ft) and is generally accepted.

Sunset glow on Everest, from Tibet Base Camp

Early ascents

After a reconnaissance mission in 1921 and a failed attempt in 1922, George Mallory returned to Everest in 1924. Team mates Edward Norton and Howard Somervell tried to summit without oxygen, but they turned around after Norton had climbed to 8573m (28,126ft). On June 8, Mallory and Sandy Irvine went for the summit, with supplementary oxygen. They were last seen on the summit ridge by Noel Odell, but it is unclear exactly where. Mallory's body was discovered in 1999, but neither Irvine nor their cameras have yet been found. Although they clearly died on their way down, there is continuing controversy about whether or not they had summited.

A Swiss team came very close in 1952, when Raymond Lambert with sherpa Tenzing Norgay turned back at about 8595m (28,210ft). Tenzing returned the next year for his seventh and most famous Everest expedition, under the leadership of John Hunt. Charles Evans and Tom Bourdillon made the first ascent of the South Summit, but lack of time and oxygen turned them back. Two days later, on 29 May 1953, Tenzing Norgay and Edmund Hillary reached the top of the world. Whether Mallory preceded them is irrelevant: they were the first to summit and come back alive.

Wang Fu-chou, Chu Yin-hua and Konbu (or Gonpa), 3 members of a huge Chinese team, were the first to summit from the Tibet side on 25 May 1960. On 8 May 1978, Reinhold Messner and Peter Habeler summited without using supplementary oxygen. Many scientist had previously thought this impossible. The Washburn map gives concise details of many significant expeditions and first ascents by various routes: see page 95.

Statistics and disasters

Whilst 1982 and 1988 were lethal years (10 and 11 deaths respectively), the mountain's killer reputation was confirmed after the 1996 season in which 15 climbers died. Described in many books, those deaths also were linked with the era of commercial expeditions and controversy.

The number of Everest climbers has increased sharply in recent years. Since 1969 there have been fatalities in every year but one (1977). On average, 5 climbers died each year for the last 40.

Including the 2007 season, a total of 210 deaths have been reported on Everest since 1922. Although the annual number of fatalities has

risen since 1996, the much-quoted ratio of deaths to summiteers has been decreasing. In 2007, the ratio was about 1 in 20 (5.7%). (This statistic compares the number of climbers who died, whether they summited or not, with climbers who summited and survived.)

By the end of 2007, the summit had been reached 3681 times, by 2422 separate climbers (many of whom made several ascents) from 73 countries. 617 Nepali summiteers (mostly sherpas) account for 42.5% of these 1564 summits. Nepali climbers also account for 65 of the 210 deaths (31%). More summits were made in the years 2003-2007 than in all years to 2002.

Memorial to all those who have died, Pheriche

Climbing Everest is a perfect reason to visit these wonderful places. Immerse yourself in a region that is financially poor, but culturally very rich. Even if you never set foot on Everest, your life will be enriched by your visit.

Tibet is the highest region on earth, the altitude of its plateau being over 4000m. Whilst large parts are cold, dry and dusty, five of the biggest rivers in Asia start here, supplying water for one in three of the world's citizens. Tibet's history, boundaries and status are all very controversial. It has never been accepted as independent by any other country. Although its spiritual leader, the Dalai Lama, recognizes the political rule of China, the western world does not accept the status of the 'Tibet Autonomous Region', which comprises less than half of historic Tibet.

Tibet was invaded by the Chinese army in 1950, and following upheavals, the 14th Dalai Lama fled to Dharamsala (India) in 1959. The Chinese persecution and cultural attacks on Tibetans have persisted ever since, and were widely reported by the world's media in 2008 when Beijing hosted the Olympics. Tibetan culture is disappearing fast and, outnumbered by Han Chinese, they have become an ethnic minority. They can be arrested for showing a Tibetan flag or even for owning a photo of the Dalai Lama.

Southern neighbour Nepal is landlocked between India and China. Of its population of 29.5 million, nearly one-third live in poverty, with agriculture providing a livelihood for 76% of Nepalis. Officially a Hindu state, about 80% of Nepalis are Hindu, yet Buddhism seems much more visible in the Khumbu valley. After centuries of rule by hereditary premiers or monarchs, a rising in 1996 led by Maoists was followed by civil war, protests and a peace accord in 2006. In May 2008, parliament declared Nepal a democratic federal republic at its first meeting. The King vacated his throne in June and parliament elected Nepal's first President in July.

While there are humid plains in the south, the mighty Himalaya run right across its northern part and Nepal boasts eight of the world's ten highest mountains. There are many wonderful treks, for example the famous Annapurna circuit, or in the Langtang National Park close to the capital, Kathmandu.

The sherpas

The sherpa people came from Tibet several centuries ago and live in the mountain regions, mostly in the east. Their sherpa language is closer to Tibetan than Nepali. They live off the land in rugged terrain with few if any roads. Most live at altitudes above 3000m/10,000ft, and they are naturally well acclimatized.

Because of their physical strength and knowledge of the mountains, sherpas are in demand to work as porters and guides on Himalayan expeditions. Nowadays, the name *sherpa* has been generalised to mean *porter*. This is confusing because not all sherpas work as porters and not all porters are ethnically sherpa. Most sherpa guides are well respected climbers and some have summited many times. Without their support, few expeditions would be successful.

Heavily laden sherpa porter

Sherpas often use the seven days of the week to name their newborn babies, irrespective of gender. Depending which day they were born, many are called Nima, Dawa, Mingma, Lhakpa, Phurba, Pasang, and Pemba (Sunday to Saturday). To avoid confusion, ask also for their second name or hometown.

Buddhism and *puja* ceremonies

Buddhism is the main religion in the region, and you'll see many *mani* stones and walls, prayer wheels, and *chortens* along the trail, with prayer flags tied to the bridges and in the camps. Try to learn about Buddhism before you go. It's traditional to rotate prayer wheels clockwise and to walk clockwise around *mani* stones; never sit or stand on them. The mantra of compassion inscribed on them is *Om mani padme hum* ('Hail to the jewel in the lotus').

Prayer flags are printed in five colours, and are left flying until they disintegrate, carrying the prayers up to heaven and transforming the five negative emotions into the five Buddhist wisdoms. *Gompas* are Buddhist temples, often with smaller structures nearby. A *chorten* is a hemispherical shrine on a square base; above it is a tower with the eyes of the all-seeing Buddha, and inside are religious relics. A large chorten is called a *stupa*.

Sherpas will not ascend the higher parts of the mountain until after a *puja* ceremony is held in camp. Take along all your climbing gear to place by the altar, a pile of carefully placed rocks. The Lama blesses the climbers, their gear and the expedition making ancient, long prayers for a safe return from the mountain.

Prayer flags

At the end, food is passed around. Rice as well as *tsampa* (roasted barley flour), is thrown into the air as an offering to the gods, and alcohol is offered to confuse evil spirits. Long strings of prayer flags are tied to a pole at the altar, sending their prayers in 3 or 5 directions.

Kathmandu

Everest expeditions normally start in Kathmandu, even those climbing from the Tibetan side. All operators (for both routes) are based there and you can get all supplies you need, from climbing ropes to food and porters. Nepal's only international airport, Tribhuvan, has direct daily flights from many Asian hubs.

Bouddhanath, a huge stupa

Kathmandu is well worth a visit for its own charms. Though dirty and polluted, many travellers love the chaotic mix of smells, sounds and cultures. Enjoy the hustle and bustle of the touristy Thamel district, crowded with shops, restaurants and rickshaw drivers.

Spend a day strolling towards and around the 2000-year old Swayambunath complex, (the 'Monkey Temple'), with a fine monastery and great views over the city. Be sure to see the Bouddhanath (the largest Buddhist stupa in Nepal, and a World Heritage Site) and the Hindu Pashupatinath complex, best known for its public cremations.

Lhasa

Some climbers fly to Lhasa first, then go to Tibet BC. Even if you are going overland by the regular route or climbing from Nepal, it's good to visit the capital of Tibet. Its altitude (3650m/11,975ft) will help with acclimatization, and it's an interesting place. There are regular flights and organized tours from Kathmandu.

Visit the famous Jokhang Temple and the Potala and Norbulingka Palaces of the Dalai Lama. Though most of the Buddhist culture is now replaced with Chinese and nobody is allowed to speak freely, in the Barkhor area you can still catch some glimpses of the original culture of the former highest capital in the world.

Potala from Jokhang

Currencies

Nepal uses rupees (NPR) with about 80 per US $1 (in November 08). In touristy parts, US dollar notes may be accepted, and the Euro is also being discovered. China uses the Yuan (CNY), with about 7 to $1. Beware of unofficial moneychangers who may use fake notes or give poor rates. It helps to have US dollars in small denominations, and credit/debit cards as backup.

Time zones

Nepal Time is GMT +5.45, but all of China uses Beijing Time (GMT+8), leading to a loss of 2¼ hours when you cross the border at Friendship Bridge. In your expedition make sure that *everybody* (including the sherpas) uses **either Nepal time or China time**, and not a mixture. Time confusion can lead to various frustrations, or even, higher up, to real danger.

Power supply and telephoning

Electricity in both Nepal and China is nominally 220v, 50Hz, but voltage can fluctuate and interruptions are not unusual. You should carry voltage converters (if your appliances need 110v) and plug adaptors to suit your destinations.

In the Khumbu valley, many tea houses rely on solar power and it's normal to have to pay to recharge batteries. Plugs in Nepal are generally round-pin, either with two or three pins. In Tibet, plugs may be round-pin with 2 or 3 pins, or 3 flat pins set at an angle.

To dial Nepal and Tibet from another country, dial the international access code (usually 00 but 011 from the US) then the country code (977 for Nepal, or 86 for China), followed by the number.

3·1 Kathmandu to Base Camp

The journey to Base Camp begins with a drive of 120km to reach the Tibet border, which takes about 4 hours due to regular police and army checks *en route*. No vehicles can cross the border (**Friendship Bridge**). Keep hold of your valuables, and have your visa papers ready. Register at the far side of the bridge, then continue up the road. Get into your next vehicle with your personal luggage while the expedition gear is loaded into Chinese trucks.

The customs checkpoint is at the beginning of **Zhangmu** where all luggage, passports and visas will be checked. Zhangmu is at 2200m (7200ft), and its winding main street is lined with bars, shops, hotels, restaurants, internet cafes and a cash machine. All expeditions overnight here, in both directions.

Next day the journey continues upwards over narrow muddy roads through wild and wonderful landscapes. Enjoy the moist air and the last trees you'll see for 4-5 weeks. You gain altitude very quickly, rising over 1500m to **Nyalam** (3750m/12,300ft). Accommodation here is simple and cold: you'll need a down jacket, gloves and hat. Help your acclimatization by spending two nights here, meanwhile drinking plenty and making a hike or two.

Above Nyalam, you approach the barren, eroded Tibetan plateau. The road rises to the Thang La pass at 5050m (16,570ft), filled with prayer flags and scarves. Look for a striking mountain about 40km to your south-west: at 8027m, Shishapangma (or *Xixabangma*) is the only 8000+ peak that lies wholly in Tibet.

After a slightly lower pass, the Lalung La, you descend to the arid plateau. Another 70km of dusty roads will take you to **Old Tingri** (also *Tingri* or *Dingri*), little more than a main street with shops and restaurants. On your right is the huge white massif of Cho Oyu (8201m), the sixth highest mountain in the world. If you can spot a rocky triangle to its left, poking above the clouds, it's Chomolangma (Everest)!

Low-budget Everest expeditions stay here for the night, others continue 50km or so to **New Tingri** (*Xegar*). Ask your organizer where you will stay in advance. Both Tingris are at about 4300m, but New Tingri is cleaner and quieter, with a hotel 7km from the town.

New Tingri offers various acclimatization hikes, assuming you spend a spare day there. Walking into town takes about 1½ hours. Its old

> **Trekking to Tibet Base Camp**
> From Old Tingri you can instead hike to BC, although few climbers do it. This high-altitude trek through simple villages and fields with yaks and sheep takes about four days and crosses the Nam-La pass at 5250m (17,220ft). You can hire a guide or even yaks in Tingri, but need to be mainly self-sufficient at high altitude. The route uses the same bumpy trails as most of the expedition vehicles, and meets the main road about 20km before BC.

Base Camp, with Everest behind

part has the beautiful old Shegar Chöde Monastery, near the foot of the hill. Follow the clockwise spiral track uphill after you pass through the wall, avoiding other tracks which are unsafe. It takes about an hour to hike up to the thousands of prayer flags on top, rewarded on clear days by views of Everest.

At the turn-off, you leave the Friendship Highway, soon stopping at the control point where permits are checked. An endless series of switchbacks takes you to the highest pass: Pang-La at 5150m (16,900ft). When cloud-free, you'll see four of the world's highest mountains on the horizon: Makalu, Lhotse, Everest and Cho Oyu.

More switchbacks bring you down to the small village of Tashi Dzom (also known as *Zhaxizom*, *Peruche* or *Padu*). Tashi is a great place to return to rest just before a summit attempt. It is only 50km from BC, but 1200m lower and takes about 2 hours by car: its thick air feels great after weeks at altitude. You can walk around town or visit the old red monastery halfway up the hill, a 30-45 minute hike to the west.

The road follows the river and passes some more settlements. Then it steepens and after 50km you will suddenly see buildings and a GSM mast. This is Rongbuk (or *Rongphu*), home of the highest monastery and hotel in the world, with wonderful views of Everest.

Tourists are not allowed to drive any further, but with a climbing permit you can continue the final 8km by vehicle. After a few switchbacks up the old moraine, you reach an open field with many yaks and assorted tents. This is the tourist part of BC, also known as Chinatown. The stone building on the small hill houses the Liaison Officer (LO) and his staff. The real BC lies behind – a huge flat area with Everest 16 km in the distance.

The Landcruisers and trucks continue over some bumpy tracks all the way to the camps in the back. Some expeditions stay on the LO side for easy access to services, others prefer to stay further from Chinatown for safety and privacy. They make camp about 900m ahead, close to the snout of the old Rongbuk Glacier.

3 The Tibet route
3·2 Base Camp to Intermediate Camp

Altitude gained	**600m (1970ft)**
Time up	**first time 5-7 hours, thereafter 4-5 hours**
Time down	**first time 4-5 hours, thereafter 3-4 hours**
Summary	**This section is a straightforward, non-technical hike, but several rises and falls make the last section tiring.**

The trek from BC to ABC is very long, at first usually split into two days with a stop in Intermediate Camp (IC). Once fully acclimatized, you should be able to go straight from BC to ABC (or at least from ABC down to BC). Larger teams will maintain an IC all season for emergencies and extra service.

The tracks vary quite a bit, year on year and even during the season as glaciers move and melt, creating new hazards and options. However, the overall direction is clear, and the tracks are more worn (lighter in colour) than the surrounding rock. If in doubt, just look for the most obvious signpost on the valley floor: yak dung. When there is snow and no fresh yak tracks, look for rock-covered prayer flags or 'stone men' – small man-made piles of rocks.

Depending on the location of your BC, you may have to cross the wide plateau first or just skirt the glacier eastwards. When coming from the LO side, you need to take care when crossing the small river: it's easy to get your feet wet, which may later lead to blisters or even frostbite.

Aim for the left (east) side of the glacier and you will find the sandy tracks. Every now and then the track splits, usually because of the yak trains, but they soon merge. Generally the track alternates between the side of the glacier and the bottom of the moraine.

The first 3km is overall fairly level, and you gain only about 100m of altitude in almost a straight line south-south-easterly. First time around, this section will seem endless, but later you'll be able to hike it at full speed, reducing your time from about 1½ hours to half that.

When reaching the obvious point where the East Rongbuk Glacier merges with the main flow, the path goes up steeply to the left. Take it easy here, walking slowly but steadily. Listen for oncoming yaks and move aside in time to let them pass. Some sections are exposed and narrow, and can be slippery due to snow patches. Once you have completed the sharp turn you'll be walking eastwards. Everest is now hidden behind the Changtse massif and the track levels out again at about 5500m (18,050ft).

This open area is often referred to as 'Yak Camp'. The Yak herders usually take a break here and some teams camp on one of the flat spots. Unfortunately the yaks also use the walled spaces to drop their dung, so it is messy. It is still a good place to have lunch. On your first time up, you may want to turn back and descend to BC from here.

After a little uphill section, the track levels out again. As the river on your right comes up to your level, you walk alongside it for a while. Depending on conditions, the river and small lakes may still be frozen and snow-covered, in which case the track may go over them in a straight line. Later in the season, you walk around the small lakes, but the route may have changed again before you head back down to BC.

In the fall and late season, the lakes will melt much more. If needed, there is an alternative route: cross the river when possible (usually it flows underneath part of the glacier) and head south, over some moraine hills to the other side of the glacier. There lies another track, joining the valley track further on.

After a long flat part, which in parts almost resembles a beach with fine sand, you climb again, having crossed diagonally towards the south side of the glacier. In the distance you will already be able to see the big white icy triangles, the 'ice sharks', marking IC. Although you are close to the camp, this last part is tough and takes at least an hour: many small hills need to be crossed, taking lots of energy.

Base Camp
5200

Yak Camp
5500

Intermediate
Camp 5800

IC is quite spread out and most camps can be seen only once you are very close. If you are unguided, make sure you know which side of the central moraine your camp is. Some climbers have walked right past their camps, because all spots are off the main track.

The main commercial camps are just on the other side of the central moraine, close to the 'ice sharks'. This means a very tough final climb up the icy moraine and down the other side. Some other camps use the section south-west of the moraine. For them, don't cross the moraine but head straight on and continue up the small hills on the Changtse side of the valley.

The track up the moraine is usually very slippery as the thin layer of rocks covering the hard blue glacier ice gets eroded quickly as the season progresses. Take good care and use poles. The river at the bottom of this slope will melt and swell, needing some river-crossing skills and advanced rock-hopping.

Giant 'ice sharks' are the landmark for IC

57

Altitude gained	**600m (1970ft)**
Time up	**first time 6-8 hours, thereafter 3-5 hours**
Time down	**first time 4-5 hours, thereafter 2-3 hours**
Summary	**This section is a straightforward hike with some icy, slippery sections, but altitude will make the last part seem endless.**

From both IC locations, the start is tough because you have to climb to the very top of the central moraine. Afterwards, the route is quite gradual and easy to follow: just stay on top for about 3km, walking almost due south-south-east on the rocky moraine between the icy glaciers.

Near the end of this section, the track moves to the left (east) side of the moraine and down a little until you are level with the ice. Cross a small river (usually frozen) and after climbing a few metres back up again, the area will open up. This entire section can be very slippery due to unexpected bare blue ice, so take great care.

The open area is sometimes referred to as Changtse Camp: you can ascend Everest's smaller cousin Changtse (7543m) from here, where

Yaks among the ice sharks, en route for ABC

Intermediate Camp
5800

Changtse Camp
6050

Advanced Base
Camp 6400

the Changtse Glacier (to your right) merges with the East Rongbuk. This is halfway to ABC in horizontal distance, but a little less than that vertically. There are many good places to have lunch if it is not too windy, and you may find some yak-herders selling soft drinks.

Continue straight along the clear track south-easterly, passing a huge ice-slab coming down from Changtse. Depending on the season, you may have to cross or go around some small lakes. The smaller hills may be icy, although crampons aren't needed. Usually there's one big crack in the glacier which must be circumnavigated by going down and around its left (eastern) side. Like Changtse BC, this area will also be wet at the end of the season, with many small lakes and ponds affecting the route.

Basically you have to go all the way around Changtse. As soon as you seem to head straight into the ice-sharks and Everest appears again, the track will make another 90° turn to the south-west. It isn't much further, but you still have to ascend about 200m so it will feel very tough, especially the first time. Once you are in Changtse's shadow, the temperature can drop like a stone, so carry your warm clothes and aim to arrive before 17.00. Even though ABC is close, protect yourself from hypothermia, frostbite and AMS, and keep well hydrated.

Soon you will see the first tents, many of them belonging to climbers who have come to climb Lhakpa Ri, the 7045m (23,114ft) high mountain to your left. Everest ABC is still a bit further and higher. If you are unguided, make sure you know how to recognize your team's camp as it can take an hour from the beginning of ABC to the highest tents. When you are tired and AMS-prone, the last thing you need is to waste time looking for your kitchen tent.

ABC is a big place, and the best spots will have been taken by the large operators. If you are going to make your own camp, don't be tempted to camp too close to Changtse. Although it's sheltered, there's a lot of rockfall from the mountain.

3·4 Advanced Base Camp to North Col

Altitude gained	**660m (2160ft)**
Time up	**first time 5-7 hours, thereafter 3-5 hours**
Time down	**first time 3-5 hours, thereafter 2-3 hours**
Summary	**A short hike and a glacier walk, followed by the most rewarding snow and ice climbing on Everest.**

The North Col is the saddle joining Changtse to Everest (on the left in the photograph below). The weather is very changeable here, so prepare for all conditions. Always bring your down jacket and windproof trousers and jacket, as well as warm gloves.

Try to do some acclimatization hikes to NC before actually sleeping there, to prepare for the large altitude gain. Go to the base of the ropes, or even all the way up, returning to ABC to sleep. Once you are on your summit bid, pack extra carefully: don't forget anything vital such as your headtorch, down suit, oxygen regulator or goggles.

Advanced Base Camp, with the North Col behind

Follow the meandering track through the upper ABC camp spots. The area between Changtse and the glacier narrows and you walk only a few metres from the ice. Just when you think you can go no further, heading straight for a rock face, the track turns left, up the glacier. First time around, this section can take 1½ hours. Later this time should decrease to about half. If not, you probably aren't fit or acclimatized enough to climb any higher.

About 10m higher up is 'Crampon Point', a little plateau with several blue drums filled with crampons and ice axes. Most belong to the sherpas who make several trips up here to build the route and carry supplies. It's wiser to take your crampons with you to and from ABC – to leave them here is to risk mistakes or theft.

Start wearing your crampons from here. You may not need them before the fixed ropes, but the next 100 metres are usually icy and there are a few small crevasses ahead. Follow the tracks over the rocks and hard ice until you emerge on to the East Rongbuk Glacier. It's fairly flat here and most people don't rope up. Head to the right and follow the crampon marks for about 30-45 minutes toward the start of the fixed ropes.

Walk steadily, looking back regularly to note the return route. There may be some small marker sticks to help. It's much harder to find the correct exit from the glacier when coming down. Especially in white-out conditions, there is a risk of descending too low, where large crevasses lurk.

The route changes slightly each year, so the description below is just a guideline. Use the fixed rope techniques described on p42, moving slowly but steadily. Never leave the ropes: they are there to help protect you from crevasses and falls.

It's mostly not too steep, but very tiring, especially if the sun is out. Despite the altitude (6650m), it can be extremely hot as you bake in a reflector oven. Any cooling wind tends to be blocked by the wall of ice in front. Stay covered up, lest you get seriously sunburned.

Drink plenty, and try to minimize sweating. Conditions can change suddenly and the weather usually approaches from the other side.

The first part is a continuous straight climb that gains about 150m quickly. When it flattens out, take a break: the next section is short (about 10m vertical) but usually very steep if not vertical. The ice can be blue and hard, so you need good crampons.

After this section you'll need another rest. Continue between some old avalanche debris to cross a small crevasse, usually via a small ladder. Then the route turns right again and you cross a small open valley, still in the avalanche zone, which gets much steeper at the far end. Take a break before you turn left to climb a short steep section, which can be about 5m vertical if there's not much snow.

From here it can take another hour to reach camp. The route steepens again and the last slope seems endless, with a near-vertical final part. Usually steps are cut to make ascent and descent easier: step carefully so as to avoid damage. Once it flattens out again, you may see some tents, but not yet the main North Col Camp. Turn left to cross another crevasse, usually spanned by a long ladder or even two tied together.

Ascend the last slope to emerge on to a large plateau, filled with tents. The huge ice shelf above gives protection from the Nepali winds. In camp, use common toilet areas to limit contamination, as all water needs to be melted from snow. Bigger expeditions have a toilet tent close to the ice shelf where there is a hidden bergschrund: take care! Don't 'go' over the edge towards ABC, where a slip would be fatal.

Climbers approaching the start of the fixed
ropes at 6600m, leading toward the North Col

Altitude gained	**590m (1940ft)**
Time up	**first time 5-7 hours, thereafter 3-5 hours**
Time down	**first time 2-3 hours, thereafter 1-2 hours**
Summary	**Hard slog over a seemingly endless series of snowy hills, followed by easy scrambling up an exposed ridge**

The section between North Col (or Camp 1) and High Camp (Camp 3) at 8250m/27,070ft may be split into two or three sections. The advantage of making two camps in between is a slower ascent and more rest. However, to minimize your time in the Death Zone (see p14) we will describe our preference – to make only one camp *en route* to High Camp, at about 7650m/25,100ft.

You will climb on a ridge all day and the wind can hit you at full force. If you are going up an acclimatization hike only, you may get away with just a down jacket, otherwise a full down suit and warm gloves are usually needed. Most climbers start the use of O_2 when leaving NC or in Camp 2, or somewhere in between.

From your tent, clip into the rope leading through camp and continue up until you have passed the big protective ice shelf. It can be very windy here, so dress accordingly. You then go down a little but stay on the rope until you reach the actual North Col. Even where the walking is easy, there can be crevasses and cornices.

Camp at the North Col, 7060m

The next 500m of ascent is a straightforward slog over a few hills, in an almost straight line. Every hill is a bit steeper and higher than its predecessor. On top of the last and highest hill, the area just before the rocks is relatively flat. This is the first camp made by teams who opt to make two intermediate camps between NC and High Camp, at 7500m/24,600ft. All sites are steep, rocky and very exposed, but there are many small spots for a single tent.

Head slightly to the right of the ridge and climb on to the rocks. Keep your crampons on as there may be snow and ice patches. The ridge is only at about 45°, but the altitude will make you gasp. The last 200m up will take another 1-2 hours.

When arriving at camp, resist the urge to go to sleep immediately. Instead, fire up the stoves to re-hydrate and eat as much as you can. Let your team leader know how you feel and about your plans. Sleep with an oxygen flow of 0.5 l/min. Ear plugs may help to calm your nerves at night, drowning the loud tent-flapping noise.

Lone tent perched on the ridge, Camp 2

65

Altitude gained	**600m (1970ft)**
Time up	**4-7 hours**
Time down	**1-3 hours**
Summary	**A high altitude rock hike with some snowfields, taking you to the highest campsite in the world**

Most people set an average oxygen flow of about 2 l/min while climbing from Camp 2 and upward: check your system while in camp. Hydrate at breakfast and melt two extra litres for today's hike. Continue the meandering trail through the different camps. The terrain is easy, but the altitude is against you. Weather can be very changeable here as clouds come and go, alternating between sunshine and chilly snow-laden winds.

At about 7900m the route flattens out a bit and the density of tents increases again. This is the second campsite for those who use two intermediate camps. The trail leaves the ridge here and heads up diagonally onto the mighty North Face. Follow the line over a natural trail: some small and some wider ledges lead to a large snowfield, to the left of you. You have just crossed the 8000m line.

After climbing the gently sloping, 100m-high snowfield and after the rocks to its right, you arrive at a small flat space where you can rest. Some even camp here, though space is limited to 1-2 tents, so don't count on it. After a further diagonal traverse you will arrive at the bottom of yet another snowfield. Go left and head straight up.

Just when you will start wondering where the camp might be, you will notice bright colours in the snow. The camp here is spread out over a large area, with upper tents 50m higher than the lower ones. Almost all the spots are away from the fixed line, so walk carefully and always use your axe and crampons when going to visit team mates or to relieve yourself.

Camp 2
7650
Traverse
7900
High Camp
8250

Rest and recover, but do not sleep: start collecting and melting snow immediately. Assess how you feel and confirm it with a team mate if possible. If you feel strong enough to go up another 600m, contact your team leader for the latest weather forecasts and to discuss your summit and oxygen plan again. Look outside to check the weather yourself and look at the rope and route carefully and repeatedly. Try to memorize the features: when you go there a few hours later, it will be pitch dark.

If you still feel good after you have re-hydrated and filled all your other bottles and maybe eaten something, try to rest or sleep using 0.5 l/min oxygen flow. If you feel bad after all, go down now, while you can still reach Camp 2 during daylight. Make sure you have agreed the exact departure time and whether this is on Nepal or Tibet time: see p51.

View north-west from High Camp, near sunset

3·7 High Camp to the summit

Altitude gained	**600m (1970ft), and descend as far as possible**
Time up	**6-12 hours**
Time down	**3-7 hours (to High Camp)**
Summary	**The longest, toughest day so far, with steep snow, exposed ledges and technical rock-climbing in extreme cold; keep reserves for the dangerous descent**

Get up at least two hours before the agreed departure time (which is usually around midnight, Tibet time) in order to melt snow or heat water for breakfast and to dress fully. Use a fresh pair of socks and make sure your feet are warm and dry and that your inner boots have dried and warmed up in your sleeping bag. Check your gear (including battery level of radio and headtorch) and other contents of your summit pack. Re-check your oxygen bottles. Just before you leave, replace the one you used to get to camp (and for resting so as to start with a full bottle.

If applicable, communicate with your team mates by radio about the exact moment you will set off. Stay inside your tent until everybody is fully ready, drinking more. Waiting outside without moving would rapidly cause frostbite. When all are ready, go outside, clip into the fixed rope and start climbing with your team.

The fixed rope continues straight on to a steepening snowfield. At the end of the snowfield you will hit a 6m/20ft wall, which will take a lot of effort to surmount and which is scratched with crampon marks. If you cannot recover from this easily, turn back now as the 'Steps' ahead are much more demanding.

This is the entrance to the 'Exit Cracks', a series of gullies and rock ledges, leading quite naturally to the summit ridge at 8500m/27,900ft. The Cracks are never really steep and the biggest problem may be the old. frayed fixed ropes from previous years. If there is any moonlight, you will be able to see right down the apparently vertical 3600m Kangchung Face of Everest.

High Camp
8250

First Step
8550

Second Step
8625

Third Step
8700

Summit
8848

The 2000m vertical drop of the North Face is not that steep, but the exposure is extreme and the ropes and anchors may be worn or loose. Try to keep your balance on the narrow traverse without testing their strength. The entire section leading to the Second Step has many small rock ledges where you need to down-step and up-step many times. In the pitch dark it can be unnerving to step down on to scratched downwards-sloping ledges leading to nowhere.

Check your oxygen and timing on the ridge. If you've used more than half a bottle, or taken more than 2½ hours to get here, *seriously* consider turning around. To continue, turn right and follow the fixed ropes, traversing along the summit ridge. You pass a small overhang, almost a cave, where the lower legs of an Indian climber may still be sticking out of the snow. He has become a landmark known as 'Green Boots'.

The route continues fairly level while the ridge steepens. The dark rocky shape emerging in front of you is the First Step. This isn't very steep, and the main part is only about 12m high. At sea level, it would be an easy scramble, but in the dark at 8550m it is very tough. Usually the main track ascends on the left side of the gully, depending on the snow. Once you pass the big boulders at the start, it gets easier. Don't go too fast lest you get dizzy and lose your footing.

Once on top of the First Step, you are on the summit ridge again. Traverse carefully just below it (always on its north side) until you reach, and perhaps rest at, the 'Mushroom Rock' formation. Many climbers change their oxygen bottle here, leaving the half-empty bottle to be picked up on the way down. This saves weight and makes sense if you have two further full bottles left for your summit bid. If you have only one, you are gambling with high stakes. From here it can take more than 8 hours to reach the summit and return, but 8 hours is all you can expect from one full 4-litre bottle at 2 l/min flow.

The infamous Second Step

The track traverses just below the ridge, ending at the foot of the Second Step. Reaching the ladder is difficult because climbing the lower part of this Step takes so much physical and mental strength. Stow your ice axe so you can use both hands, but stay attached to the newest fixed rope with your jumar. All the ropes are heavily used, and none are reliable. Try to avoid pulling hard on the ropes, using good technique instead.

ladder →

High Camp
8250

First Step
8550

Second Step
8625

Third Step
8700

Summit
8848

The 1.5m pile of smaller rocks can be surmounted easily as it has many cracks for your crampon points. Don't go straight into the chimney, but turn right instead and work your way up and around the smooth rocks. At first some tiny ledges on the right side help you to get up. When going down, abseiling is usually the easiest option, if a good, untangled fixed rope is available.

Slowly step up the rungs as high as possible and then step off the ladder, placing your crampon tips on the tiny ledges to your right. One more carefully placed left-foot step, combined with a pull on the ropes, should take you quickly over the slight overhang. It's harder when descending: you step backwards over the edge, looking straight down towards the Rongbuk Glacier and some corpses at the foot of the Step. You may already be exhausted: if you can't find your footing quickly, step back up again to regain strength before trying again.

If you are fit, the entire Step can be climbed in less than 15 minutes, but most people take longer, resulting in traffic jams. Some climbers become frostbitten after having to wait motionless for 1-2 hours. Many climbers turn up their oxygen flow for the Step: don't do this too soon, or your supply may be depleted too fast.

Makalu, from the Third Step at sunrise

71

The route to the Third Step is much easier and relatively flat, in a straight line along the exposed ridge. If snow conditions are good, it takes only a few minutes to step up the natural path through this 10m-high pile of rocks. Enter from the left and head up to the top right, where it flattens out again. With care, climbers can even pass each other, so there should be no bottleneck. When going down, you can usually simply step down, facing out if you are confident.

Above is an interesting short curvy section over a snowy ridge, only a few steps from the sheer drop into Tibet. Then the way opens up again and you are at the bottom of the Snow Pyramid, the last main slope. If you are running out of oxygen or energy, turn around here. It may look close, but the summit is still at least an hour away, more probably 2-3 hours, plus extra descent time. You still have about 150m/500ft of altitude to gain, plus a long traverse.

The track starts straight up the 45° snow and ice field and then curves to the right until it ends horizontally at the base of some rocks. Fresh snow can make the ascent tough and much longer, but normally the slope is blown clean and the steps are easy. The rocks mark the beginning of a short, dangerous section: the rock traverse.

This part is very exposed, the ropes are usually in bad condition and the tracks rocky, slippery and narrow. Sudden gusts of wind can hit hard, throwing you off balance. If possible, wait for a quiet spell before heading to the end of the traverse. Make a 160° turn and head up the easier rocks until you reach another snowfield.

Turn right here and walk on easy ground to the top of the snowfield, which is a false summit. The real one is a further 150m/500ft ahead. The last section traverses between some giant cornices and a rocky slope, so take care, especially if there is no fixed rope. Soon you will see some colours to the left – remainders of prayer flags and maybe some clothing. Turn left to ascend the final 10m over a few switchbacks to reach the summit. You are on top of the world!

Be sure to keep track of time while on the summit, and to monitor the weather. Inform your team leader by radio, but don't phone home until you can report your safe descent. Reaching the summit marks only the halfway point.

Take as many pictures as you can while watching your time. Try to show faces in photos of yourself and your team mates, ideally taking a few without oxygen mask and goggles. Aim to have the subject sitting down, with other mountains in the frame, so the image is recognizably Everest. Batteries and electronics fail easily in extreme cold, but a cheap single-use film camera needs no batteries.

A queue of climbers may be waiting to take summit photos. Everybody worked hard to get here, so be patient and stay calm. If you change to your last oxygen bottle, be sure to take down the empty one. Falling bottles almost killed climbers coming up the North Face a few years ago. Don't leave anything on the summit: it will blow away, and your memorabilia will become other people's litter. Leave only footprints and take only images.

You may notice climbers coming up from the other side. Don't be tempted to follow down the wrong side! It may sound impossibly stupid, but up there your brain doesn't work so well.

Summit view, with Rongbuk Glacier at right

3·9 Descent and return

The toughest part is yet to come: getting down safely. You need to get out of the Death Zone quickly. High Camp is too dangerous: try to descend to Camp 2, ideally to North Col or even ABC. Every step down increases your chances of survival.

Follow the same route down as you came up. Your legs will be tired and long stretches may make you dizzy. Take care on the rock traverse, and avoid slipping on the snowfield.

Read pages 71-2 for hints on descending the Second and Third Steps. Most people abseil down the First Step, but make sure the rope runs free all the way and that you are still strong enough to brake it. Otherwise it's safer to downclimb instead. Remain attached to the rope, but avoid getting your crampons caught in the ropes or your clothes. It can be very tempting to sit down, rest and take a little nap, but don't: it might be the last nap you ever take. Stay awake and keep going steadily.

Collect all gear and trash when passing the camps. Rehydrate before continuing: melt some more snow if you've run out of fluids. Keep your team informed of your location, plans and how you feel. Accept their advice over your own inclinations.

A very fit person can descend from the summit to the North Col in 5-6 hours, although most will take at least double. Drink, eat and celebrate briefly in ABC, but see your team doctor. If you have any signs of HAPE or HACE, descend to BC right away.

The long walk back to BC will pass quickly and can be done easily in a day, thanks to thicker air and the mental boost from descending. Once in BC you can celebrate with your team mates. Everyone who gets down safely is a winner, whether or not they summited.

From BC many convoys and trucks take a shortcut, the old bumpy 'direct' trail back to Old Tingri, descending to sleep in Zhangmu. Next day, change your remaining Yuan, check out at the customs and cross the Friendship Bridge to be met by your Nepalese contact. Celebrate properly once you reach the happy chaos of Kathmandu.

Looking down towards the Second Step

4 The Nepal route
4·1 Kathmandu to Tengboche

Now there's an airport at Lukla (renamed the Tenzing-Hillary Airport in 2008) most climbers fly there direct from Kathmandu to start their trek. The traditional route to the Khumbu Valley used to be to take a bus to Jiri, then trek to Base Camp over 2-3 weeks.

The Lukla flight and landing is not for the nervous flyer, and for those with enough time to spare the trek from Jiri may be preferable. The area was closed in recent years due to the civil war, but now it's open again and offers insights into rural life in Nepal, as well as the chance to get fit and acclimatized before your climb.

Many small airlines in Kathmandu offer cheap return tickets to Lukla. Flights last about 30 minutes and are frequent, mainly in the mornings, weather permitting. The planes are typically Twin Otters or other 16-20 seaters, and everybody has a window seat. Try to sit on the left (north) side for the best views.

The landing is breath-taking. The pilot steers towards the mountain on your right and it seems as if you will crash straight into it, until you notice a small airstrip perched on a ledge below, at 2840m. The runway is only 527m (1729 ft) long, built uphill at an incline of almost 20%. The combined effects of gravity and braking stop the plane only just before it hits the stone wall at the top. Flying out is almost equally exciting. Starting from the top of the runway, the pilot releases the brakes and applies full power, catapulting you over the edge of a 700-m drop to fly over the valley below.

Lukla to Phakding (2-3 hours)

A morning arrival at Lukla leaves time for breakfast and the trek down to Phakding (2610m), which may also be your first stop for the night, although many groups continue to Monjo (2840m/9320ft). It takes a couple of hours of pleasant hiking to descend 300m and then, after crossing a river, slowly to re-gain 100m. If time, hike 200m uphill on the other side of the bridge to visit the fine monastery near Phakding.

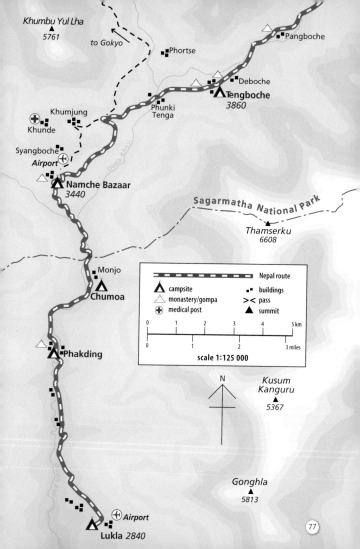

Khumbu Yul Lha
▲
5761

to Gokyo

■ Phortse

■ Pangboche

△ ■ Deboche

🛕 Tengboche
3860

Khumjung

Phunki
Tenga

✚
Khunde

Syangboche
Airport ✚

Dudh Khosi

△ ■
🛕 Namche Bazaar
3440

Sagarmatha National Park

Thamserku
▲
6608

■ Monjo

🛕 Chumoa

△
🛕 Phakding

KEY

▬▬▬	Nepal route
🛕 campsite	■ buildings
△ monastery/gompa	>< pass
✚ medical post	▲ summit

0   1   2   3   4   5 km
0   1   2   3 miles

scale 1:125 000

N

Kusum
Kanguru
▲
5367

Gonghla
▲
5813

🛕
Lukla 2840 ✚ Airport

Phakding to Namche Bazaar (4-6 hours)

The next day you stay close to the Dudh Khosi river, crossing it from time to time by suspension bridge. After 2½ hours you will pass Monjo where you pay your National Park fee. Another hour later the valley splits and you cross a huge suspension bridge. You are now very close, but the last part is tough unless you are acclimatized. A series of large switchbacks through the forest (which provides some welcome shade) takes you up the final 500m to the large village of Namche Bazaar at 3440m. Filled with lodges, internet cafes, money changers, restaurants, cheap gear and souvenirs, it's the fascinating hub of the Khumbu Valley. Saturdays are especially busy, when it hosts the regional market that gave the place its name.

Suspension bridge over the Dudh Khosi, with prayer flags

Most groups stay here two nights and make a hike on their rest day. Head up the hill north-east of the village for a great view of the valley, including Ama Dablam and Everest. You can also divert to the village of Khumjung, where Hillary built a school and a hospital. Be sure to visit the monastery with closely guarded Yeti skull.

Namche to Tengboche (4-5 hours)

Leave Namche from its east side and contour north-east around the hill, high above the Dudh Khosi river. Ignore the tracks to Khumjung and to the Gokyo valley, bearing right to keep to the main track at both junctions. You start to enjoy excellent views of the great peaks of the Khumbu: Everest, Lhotse, Nuptse and Ama Dablam.

After passing several villages and main walls, the track drops down to the river at Phunki Tenga (3250m), where the monks use water power to keep the prayer wheels turning constantly.

It's probably taken 2-2½ hours to reach Phunki, and will take as long again to reach Tengboche, despite its apparent closeness. The last part is a tough climb with 610m of altitude gain through lush forest, until finally you emerge at Tengboche (3860m). Some groups take their acclimatization day here because it's higher and quieter than Namche.

View over Namche Bazaar

Tengboche's famous Buddhist monastery was established here in 1916, but has since been destroyed and rebuilt twice. Remote and almost inaccessible until the first half of last century, it now receives some 30,000 visitors each year. It's situated on a spectacular ridge, and is well worth visiting for its services and EcoCentre: www.tengboche.org.

79

Tengboche to Pheriche or Dingboche (4-5 hours)

Continue through the forest, enjoying the fresh scents of the vegetation: this will be your last chance for several weeks. After crossing the river to its north bank you climb to reach Pangboche (3950m) within about 2-3 hours of Tengboche. It's a good place to rest and take some milk tea.

Cross a small river and continue another hour until you reach Tsuo Og, which has just a few houses. The route divides here, left for Pheriche (4275m) or right to Dingboche (4360m). If you keep going on the left of the river (crossing it 1 km ahead) you will arrive in Pheriche about 2 hours after leaving Pangboche.

Alternatively, cross the river and head uphill towards Dingboche (4360m), a larger village in a side valley leading toward Island Peak and Lhotse. You could stay two nights here and hike up the valley on the day between, or even climb Chukhung Ri (5500m), which would help you to acclimatize.

Pheriche or Dingboche to Lobuche (3-5 hours)

Leaving Pheriche, follow the valley trail for 1.5km until it branches up, slightly to the right. Continue until you cross a small bridge leading into Dughla (4620m/15,150ft), a perfect place for refreshment after 1-2 hours of hiking.

The hike from Dingboche takes about the same time. You head west, climb the sandy track up the short steep hill and head down the other side. From here you are basically walking parallel to the Pheriche variant, but 150m higher, looking over fields with great views of Cholatse and Taboche Peaks on the other side of the valley.

Ama Dablam, with chorten in foreground

Tibet / China

Nepal

Pumori
7165

Base Camp
5360

Dried Lake

N

Changri
6027

Kala Pattar
5545

Gorak Shep
5140

Khumbu Glacier

Cho La Pass
5330

← to Gokyo

Lobuche
(West)
6145

Lobuche
(East)
6119

Italian
Research
Pyramid

Lobuche
Pass
> <
5110

Lobuche
4930

*Mehra
Peak*
5817

Dzonglha

Memorials

Chola Tsho

Dughla
4620

Pokalde
5806

*Taboche
Peak*
6367

HRA clinic

Dingboche
4360

Chukhung

→ to Island Peak

Pheriche
4275

Orsho

*Ama
Dablam*
6856

Pangboche

(81)

Phortse

Sagarmatha National Park

From Dughla you head uphill for an hour over a tough rocky moraine path, gaining 200m until you reach a small pass and plateau. This is the end of the Khumbu Glacier and all the piles of rocks you see in front of you are memorials for sherpas who died on Everest. It's a sombre reminder of their hard work and the dangers they face, all to assist affluent tourists.

A few hundred metres after this pass you may notice a track leading left and up (back). This is a great variation for the return journey and a classic trek in itself: via Dzonghla and over the Cho La pass (5368m/17,611ft), then down into the Gokyo Valley, leading back to Namche. This pass is a tough trek and sees much less traffic.

For now, keep on going along a trail that's usually muddy, until you reach the collection of lodges known as Lobuche (4930m). It's a desolate and windy place with few diversions, although you can visit the Italian Pyramid research centre up the road, scramble up the glacier or climb the hills around the village. Then you can settle in front of a yak-dung-powered stove with a big bowl of soup: always remember to stay hydrated.

Lobuche to Gorak Shep (2-3 hours)

Continue along the north-west side of the Khumbu Glacier. If the sky is clear you will see the shape of Pumori looming in front of you. Climb any of the tracks up towards the U-shaped Lobuche Pass (5110m/16,765ft) and continue over a crossing of three glaciers until you reach Gorak Shep, a series of guesthouses. Like Lobuche, this settlement is here just to service the trekkers and climbers.

Most trekkers stay 1 or 2 nights in Gorak Shep (5140m), making two excursions from there: a visit to BC and a climb up Kala Pattar. As you will spend plenty of time in BC anyway, you may want to focus on Kala Pattar. If you arrive early enough, it can be climbed the same day, although the view is often obscured in the afternoons.

The hike is about a 3-hour round trip. The summit is really just an accessible part of Pumori's south ridge, at 5545m/18,190ft. Hike across the old lake, now a valley, and up the other side on sandy switchbacks. Continue upwards by going north and carefully scramble up the final exposed section. The main attraction is the view from the top, the best view of Everest's summit you can get without climbing a serious mountain: see the photograph below.

Gorak Shep to Base Camp (3-4 hours)

The section from Gorak Shep to Base Camp is strenuous in both directions. If you are just visiting BC as part of a trek, leave early because the hike down takes almost as long as uphill. The track meanders beside and then across the Khumbu Glacier. It appears closer than it is due to all the Himalayan giants around you, confusing your sense of scale.

Base Camp is located at the snout of the infamous Khumbu Icefall. Although not as jumbled as the Icefall, the BC area isn't very flat. Over the years, many good camping spots have been developed, and once the spring snow has melted it can be warm and pleasant here.

From Kala Pattar: the route starts through the Icefall, with Everest at right

Altitude gained	**590m (1930ft)**
Time up	**first time 5-8 hours, thereafter 2-5 hours**
Time down	**first time 4-5 hours, thereafter 2-3 hours**
Summary	**The Icefall is the most dangerous stretch, with exhilarating ice climbing and ladder crossings of bottomless crevasses**

The Icefall is the most treacherous part of the whole route. The Khumbu Glacier is a slow-flowing river of ice, and when its underlying rocks shift, the glacier breaks, causing crevasses. The Icefall portion lies over uneven terrain and crevasses form at all angles. Where two crevasses intersect, *seracs* form – huge, unstable blocks of ice, which can be as big as houses. The glacier's movement means that any of these blocks can topple at any moment.

There is no safe way around the Icefall, because nobody knows when a serac will fall, and the results can be deadly. Climbers can be injured or killed by ice blocks, or fall into a sudden crevasse. Aside from the Russian Roulette of the seracs, there are many 'regular' crevasses to avoid, often hidden under a thin layer of snow. Throughout your time in the Icefall, stay clipped into the fixed rope.

To help overcome these obstacles, the Ice-doctors (sherpas) try to establish a safe route using rope and ladders. Four or more ladders may be tied together to overcome the steep seracs. Altogether, several dozen ladders need to be crossed, most of them in a small portion of the Icefall. The area between the ladders is even more dangerous than the actual ladders, so always be on your guard.

To minimize accidents, go during the coldest time of day, when usually there is the least activity. Aim to start at about 4 am. The route basically heads out from BC in a straight line south-easterly. The first hour comprises a lot of small climbs interspersed with shorter, more level parts.

Then you enter the ladder zone. In the upper section, you can usually rest on a surprisingly flat part at about 5700m (18,700ft), called the 'Football Field'. In late season, this tends to break up. Different sections get various names, such as the lower and upper 'Popcorn', where a jumble of smaller, fast-moving blocks have already killed several climbers.

The upper section has the steepest walls, and the ladders can be long and crowded. Some bottlenecks have two-way routes to reduce the queues, but still you may have to wait in line. When climbing, try to clear the ladders quickly to let the next climber through. Some sections will have only dangling ropes to help you. This is where your jumar and ice-climbing technique will be needed and any gaps in your skills could prove fatal.

After the Icefall, you enter the great Western Cwm (valley) and Camp 1 is only about an hour away. There are several crevasses on

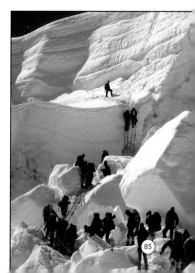

the way, so stay attached to the rope. The altitude gain (590m) means that you will go slowly, especially the first time. Climbing ladders and queueing makes it hard to find your rhythm.

Early in the season there is less ice movement, but just before and after your summit bid the warmer temperatures create extra movement and danger. Always get through this dangerous place as fast as possible, to minimize your risk.

*Queues cause delays
in the Khumbu Icefall*

Altitude gained	**450m (1480ft))**
Time up	**first time 2-4 hours, thereafter 1-3 hours**
Time down	**first time 1-2 hours, thereafter 1 hour**
Summary	**A hike through an amazingly hot valley of ice until you reach Camp 2 which is on the moraines; stay alert for crevasses at all times and use ropes for protection**

Cwm is Welsh for 'Valley'. The Western Cwm is often referred to as the 'Valley of Silence' because the wind is blocked by the huge walls of Everest and Nuptse, and all sound is absorbed by the snow. The sun's rays are reflected, creating an unbearably hot oven. Sunburn and dehydration are real risks.

At first sight this is a straight glacier hike. The horizontal distance is only about 4km/2.5mi, but you have to cross so many crevasses that it takes longer than you expect. Some crevasses are bridged by ladders, others need to be climbed down and back up again.

Camp 1, with Pumori behind at left

Camp 1
5950

Camp 2
6400

There is some steep climbing, but as the season goes on, more steps are created, making it easier. Wherever there are no fixed ropes, you should rope up with team mates, because of hidden crevasses.

The huge crevasses halfway are avoided by crossing over to the base of Nuptse on the south side of the Cwm. This section is referred to as the Nuptse Corner. You cross back again to reach Camp 2.

The camp is located on the moraine at the north side of the Western Cwm, on rocks surrounded by scree. Although this makes for easier footing in camp, it can be frustrating when hiking up the final approach.

Camp 2 is often referred to as ABC and larger expeditions have big dining tents offering relative luxury. You are camping in front of the massive South-west Face of Everest, which is so steep that from here the horizontal distance to the summit is *less* than the vertical.

Camp 2 at 6400m

Altitude gained	**750m (2460ft)**
Time up	**first time 4-7 hours, thereafter 2-4 hours**
Time down	**first time 2-3 hours, thereafter 1-2 hours**
Summary	**A straightforward ice climb up to the middle of a giant face, but any mistake could be fatal**

The first part is relatively flat and easy, it will take you from Camp 2 to the base of the Lhotse Face in about an hour. Then, after rounding a big chunk of ice, it steepens and you head up. Camp 3 is at 7150m on the Lhotse Face – the ice wall that stretches from the Western Cwm to the 8000-metre level where it becomes rocky again. You see a lot of 'bumps' and irregularities on the otherwise smooth face: these are seracs that allow space to make Camp 3. The route mostly passes this area on the left side.

The Lhotse Face dwarfs climbers at bottom left

Camp 3

Camp 2

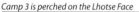

You'll pass a lot of climbers in both directions. Don't let any climbers in a hurry force you to leave the rope, not even for a minute: the risk is too great. Waterproof climbing clothes provide no friction on hard ice. If you slip here, you won't stop until you hit the bottom. Stay focused and check your rope-work. It isn't too hard technically, but don't drop your guard because there is no room for mistakes.

The slope limits the number of camping spots, but the many possible ones are spread out over a large area, mostly below protective ice-shelves which create more level ground. Your tent might seem level due to the hard work of the sherpas, but just outside the slope is still perilous. Even a simple act such as peeing can be dangerous.

Without crampons, a 10° slope on hard ice will be enough to make you fall. Always stay connected to the rope whenever possible. Otherwise at least wear crampons and carry an ice-axe.

Camp 3 is perched on the Lhotse Face

Altitude gained	**775m (2540ft)**
Time up	**first time 4-6 hours, thereafter 3-5 hours**
Time down	**2-3 hours**
Summary	**Not too steep, but on dangerous and mixed terrain you need to stay alert and use good crampon technique**

Leave camp and clip back into the main ropes up the Lhotse Face. Depending on the exact location of your camp, you climb for 1-2 hours, hugging the serac line on your right, before you start the big turn to the South Col.

This giant curve is interrupted by an interesting geological feature, called the Yellow Band. If there is not too much snow, you will notice this lighter coloured (greyish-yellow) band of limestone.

Route crossing the Yellow Band, upper Lhotse Face

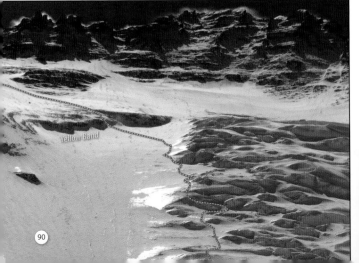

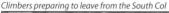

Camp 3
7150

Yellow
Band
7600

Geneva Spur
7850

South Col
7925

The rope will lead you to the weak spot where you enter the rocks after a short climb over steeper ice. Keep your crampons on and cross the rocks and the snowfield behind it, aiming for the South Col.

Before you reach the Col, you will meet another feature called the Geneva Spur, a dark rock spur on your left which fortunately does not have to be climbed at its steepest part. Basically you pass it near its top end, where it has almost sunk into the mountain.

Continue over the rocks until the South Col opens up: a wide area with snow, ice and many, many rocks of all sizes. The camp is tiny compared with the huge wall still to be climbed.

Read the notes on pp 67-8 about preparing for summit day, which apply equally here.

Climbers preparing to leave from the South Col

Altitude gained	**923m (3029ft)**
Time up	**6-12 hours**
Time down	**3-6 hours**
Summary	**By far the toughest day so far, on easy snow with an airy ridge combined with a classic rock climb, leading to the top of the world**

Leave camp over mixed ground and cross the 8000m contour. Aim straight for the left of the darkest section of rocks, located in the bottom centre of the pyramidal face. The fixed line will start here: find it, and clip in. Pass an icy section and continue straight up, following the rope up the face through a wide gully.

The roped route bends to the right over fairly easy ground. Don't be tempted to leave the rope to allow for another climber's pace: it's too dangerous. Continue until you reach 'The Balcony', a flat spot with one of the best views in the world. If it took all your strength to get here, turn back now: it only gets higher and harder. If it's daylight, look back down anyway and try to memorize the direction and location of the camp. Usually there are no ropes across the col and in a white-out it could be hard to find your way back.

The true South-east Ridge begins here and you follow it on its east side. It is wide and not exposed. If it weren't for the altitude, it would be an easy but wonderful climb with spectacular views. Stay on the right side of the ridge and the rocks you meet. Ascend the ridge at a constant pace, right up to the South Summit at 8748m/28,700ft.

You can see only false summits from here. Ask yourself if you have enough energy to keep going for several hours over harder terrain to the real summit – and enough reserve left to get back safely? Are those clouds moving in and will they turn into a storm? If in doubt, err on the safe side.

The Balcony 8400

South Summit 8748

Hillary Step 8765

Summit 8848

South Col 7925

Descend the South Summit to start the most exposed section of the entire climb – the Cornice Traverse – along a very narrow ridge over 100m long. If you have good nerves and confident legs, this could be one of the best moments of your climbing life, but one mistake and it will also be your last. Keep to the west (left) side, and beware of cornices: don't walk too close to the edge.

The Traverse leads to perhaps the most famous heap of rocks in the world: the Hillary Step – a near-vertical pile of big rocks 12m high. Usually it's partly covered in snow and ice, but sometimes it's totally bare. Snow cover makes the climbing easier, albeit exhausting at that altitude (8765m/28,760ft). The moves are not too technical, but the exposure is enormous, looking down the Kangchung Face. Enter the Step at the right side and work yourself up the fixed lines. There may be separate up- and down-lines, so beware of climbers descending the left rope.

After the Hillary Step, you are back on the ridge – not as narrow as before, but very corniced. Don't walk too close to the right (upper) edge, but stay justs below it. What looked like the top as seen from the South Summit turns out to be just another cornice, and you have to climb on. The ridge flattens out and at the end you'll see a small bump, probably with some prayer flags. From there, you suddenly look down the Tibetan side of Everest. You have reached the top of the world! See page 73 for summit advice.

Looking down the ridge from the summit

Head back down, remembering to stay away from the corniced edge. Before descending the Hillary Step, check if other climbers are coming up. If not, or if there are two ropes and sufficient space, abseil down carefully. Don't jump, or jerk the ropes: walk down slowly backwards.

Clip into the fixed line again and work yourself back along the traverse and up to the South Summit. Those few steps up will give you a good idea about how much energy you have left. From there it's an easy walk down. Go steadily and stop every now and then to drink. When arriving at the Balcony, look out for the South Col camp and memorize the direction in case of white-out.

At camp, hydrate and collect your gear. Then head down the ropes if possible, as the lower you get, the better. The rest of the descent is straightforward. If you manage to get down to Camp 2 or even Camp 1, take great care near crevasses as the afternoon heat will have weakened the snowbridges. Hydrate and eat in Camp 1, but leave very early the next morning to cross the Icefall at the coldest, least unsafe, moment.

After you have packed your gear in BC, you hike out. Most people return the same way they came in, although the side-trip via the Cho La pass (see p82) is wonderful. As you can stay anywhere, you can choose to run down in a few days or to take your time. On arrival in Lukla, don't forget to reserve your return flight for the next morning: places go quickly. Enjoy the chaos and charms of Kathmandu!

Maps and books

Everest Base Camp Adventure Map from National Geographic is probably the best map for the Nepal trek (scale 1:50,000 with Kathmandu and Nepal country maps on its obverse). It's on waterproof, tear-resistant material, available from maps.nationalgeographic.com/maps (978-1-56695-182-1 for the 2004 ed)

For the climb itself from Nepal and Tibet, Bradford Washburn's National Geographic *Mount Everest* map is unsurpassed, depicting rock, scree, moraines and crevasse fields. The whole area is shown at 1:50,000 and the obverse shows summit approaches at 1:25,000. Published by the Swiss Foundation for Alpine Research/Museum of Science, Boston (3-85515-105-9 for the 2nd ed, 1991).

So many books have been published about Everest that it's hard to select a few. *Everest: the Mountaineering History* by Walt Unsworth is the definitive, exhaustive history (Baton Wicks, 978-1898573401 for the 3rd ed, 2000).

In a very different vein, *Dead Lucky: Life after Death on Mount Everest* (Tarcher, 2008) is by Harry's friend and team-mate Lincoln Hall. This is a gripping account of his extraordinary survival in May 2006 after being left for dead overnight, at 8650m on Everest (978-1-5854-2646-1).

To understand Nepal and Tibet better, a good general guidebook is advised: the two from Lonely Planet Publications are comprehensive and reliable: *Nepal* by B Mayhew and J Bindloss (7th ed, 2006, 978-1-74059-699-2) and *Tibet* by B Mayhew et al (7th ed, 2008, 978-1-74104-569-7).

Useful websites

7summits.com/everest The author's website offers expeditions, and gives detailed information about Everest and the other seven summits. He also provides further reading suggestions and more.

www.alanarnette.com Alan Arnette's website is a great resource on some of the world's highest mountains, including Everest. Based on his climbing experiences, he provides many fine images (including ten reproduced in this book, see below), videos and route maps with overlays. Alan has used the attention his climbs have received to raise funds and awareness for the *Cure Alzheimer's Fund*: **www.curealzfund.org**

www.8000ers.com Eberhard Jurgalski's site gives detailed statistics of Everest and the other thirteen 8000+ metre peaks.

www.freetibet.org gives information about the history of the invasion and campaigns against the Chinese treatment of demonstrators and refugees.

www.nepalresearch.org provides a wealth of current information and statistics on Nepal.

Acknowledgements

The author wants to thank Alex and all of our Everest staff and clients. Thanks also to Alan, Ian, Jetta, Andy and Ivana, for making this book happen.

Photo credits

All photographs are by **Harry Kikstra** except for the following: pp 23, p37, p83, p85, p86, p87, p88, p89, p90, p91 **Alan Arnette**; p18 www.cellsalive.com; p51 **Ivana Coria** (**www.elmundoenbici.com**); p16 (all), p46, p49, p50, p78, p79, p80, p94 **Jacquetta Megarry**; p21 **Brian Spence**.

Index